Windows 95

Administration Configuration

ISBN : 2-7460-0054-7
Original edition: ISBN : 2-84072-311-5

ENI Publishing Ldt

500, Chiswick High Road
London W4 5RG

Tel: 0181 956 23 20
Fax: 0181 956 23 21

e-mail: publishing@ediENI.com
http://www.editions-eni.com

Editions ENI

BP 32125
44021 NANTES Cedex 1

Tel. (33) 2.40.92.45.45
Fax (33) 2.40.92.45.46

e-mail : editions@ediENI.com
http://www.editions-eni.com

Author : Bruno FEREC
Mega+ collection directed by Joëlle MUSSET
Translated from the French by Gillian CAIN.

Overview Chapter 1

Installation Chapter 2

Changing the configuration Chapter 3

The Plug and Play specification Chapter 4

MS-DOS applications Chapter 5

The network Chapter 6

Microsoft Exchange — Chapter 7

Mobile Computing — Chapter 8

The command prompt — Chapter 9

The registry editor Chapter 10

Troubleshooting Chapter 11

Appendices Chapter 12

Overview

A. Aims of Windows 95

Known as Chicago during while it was on the drawing board, Windows 95 was designed to achieve a set of aims:

1. Compatibility with existing software and hardware

It would have been much easier to produce an entirely new operating system without the constraints imposed on the development of Windows 95. But the new system had to take into account existing software, 16-bit applications written for previous versions of Windows (3.x) and the numerous MS-DOS applications which are still widely used. Windows 95 succeeds in meeting this challenge: any correctly developed application runs under Windows 95 without any difficulty.

A user can even fall back on restarting the computer under MS-DOS if a particularly recalcitrant application refuses to run. As soon as the application shuts down, Windows 95 restarts automatically.

2. Comfort of the user

Anyone who has used Windows 95 even for a short length of time know how simple it is to work with. The interface is designed to make using the product easy, intuitive, (even fun).

Anyone who is familiar with former versions of Windows or Apple's System 7, will get used to Windows 95 very easily.

Plug and Play technology contributes enormously to the simplicity of setting up Windows 95, not only the first time it is installed, but whenever hardware components are added.

Another time-saver: if there is a previous version of Windows on the computer, it is safe to assume that any configuration problems met during its installation have been solved. Windows 95 can use the settings of the previous version to solve configuration problems it comes up against.

Machines which are intermittently connected to devices, for instance, a portable computer which may or may not be connected to its docking station, benefit from Windows 95's capacity to redefine their configuration parameters dynamically.

One of the futuristic elements of Windows 95 is its ability to detect any infrared device in a room and to make it available for use instantly.

One of the developer's priorities was to improve access to information, both local and remote. When a user is browsing through resources, particularly in the Explorer, he hardly notices whether the resources in question are local or located on another computer in the network: access is just as easy in either case.

The interface is *docu-centric*: the emphasis is on end results. The means used to get there are not considered all-important.

For example, a user can right-click to create a new document before thinking about loading the program he or she needs to create it. This approach is in contrast to the one taken in previous versions of Windows, which were program-centred.

3. Improved performance

Previous versions of Windows (3.1 and 3.11) were based on 16-bit memory management. Windows 95, like Windows NT, is based on the API WIN32. The advantages provided by 32 bits are considerable:

Simplified developmentfor the programmer

The 16-bit segmented model of earlier Windows versions has been replace by a virtual linear address space of 4 Gb. This makes life easier for developers.

Faster running for software

One of the challenges the development team had to meet was to achieve equivalent or superior performance to a 16-bit Windows machine with 4 Mb of RAM. As more memory is added, the improvement in performance is increasingly striking.

4. Improved reliability

Although total reliability could not be achieved without breaking with existing technology (as NT does), the operating system is generally robust, much more so than the versions 3.x. This is even more evident with the new 32-bit applications.

5. Pre-emptive multitasking vs co-operative multitasking

Earlier versions of Windows exploit a type of multitasking (several applications running simultaneously) which is co-operative: each application relinquishes the processor as often as possible to let Windows process the outstanding events and so activate the other applications. This momentary suspension of activity is determined in the application by the programmer who uses the **DoEvents()** function (or similar). If the application is not well written or if an error causes it to get stuck it can disable the whole system.

Windows 95 and NT use pre-emptive multitasking. The system manages a queue of processes which are each allocated a certain amount of processor time. When that time is up, the process returns to the queue and another one is activated automatically. This means that the system is in control at all times and cannot be obstructed by an application.

Under Windows 95, 32-bit Windows applications and MS-DOS applications function with pre-emptive multitasking, whereas co-operative multitasking is used with 16-bit Windows applications, for reasons of compatibility.

B. Windows 95's place in the Microsoft range

The Microsoft operating systems currently available are as follows:

	MS-DOS 6.22
Win16	Windows 3.1
Win16	Windows for Workgroups 3.11
Win32	Windows 95
Win32	Windows NT Workstation
Win32	Windows NT Server

Windows 95 is the successor of the versions 3.x and the DOS. It does not need the DOS to run: it is a complete operating system which constitutes:

- an ideal system for an office or home platform,
- an excellent network client for Microsoft/Novell/Unix servers.

Windows NT Workstation is not in direct competition with Windows 95. NT is designed to provide a totally secure platform for confidential or exceptionally demanding applications.

NT Server is Microsoft's top-of-the-range network server platform. Windows 95 is an ideal client for it.

Both Windows 95 and NT exploit the API WIN32 and use multithreading, but only NT allows running on a multiprocessor platform.

Another important difference is that only NT runs on platforms other than INTEL (Alpha, RISC, Mips...).

C. Architecture

Windows 95 is designed around INTEL architecture and is closely linked to the 80x86 family of processors. It exploits the protected mode of 80386 and later processors, which run processes in separate rings.

Each ring corresponds to a level of privilege and security. Ring zero corresponds to privileged kernel operations, such as direct communication with hardware. The processor itself makes sure that no software can reach a section of code running in ring zero.

No software component running in ring zero must fail, otherwise the system could go down. The code must be very resistant.

Rings one and two are not used under Windows 95.

Ring three corresponds to code which needs the least privilege. At this level, the processor does not protect the segments of code. This responsibility must be assumed by the operating system.

Before it can have access to hardware, an application (running in ring three) needs to go via a process in ring zero, which may or may not validate its access to the resource. This ensures that an application can never obstruct a process running in ring zero.

↓ personal notes ↓

All applications run in ring three.

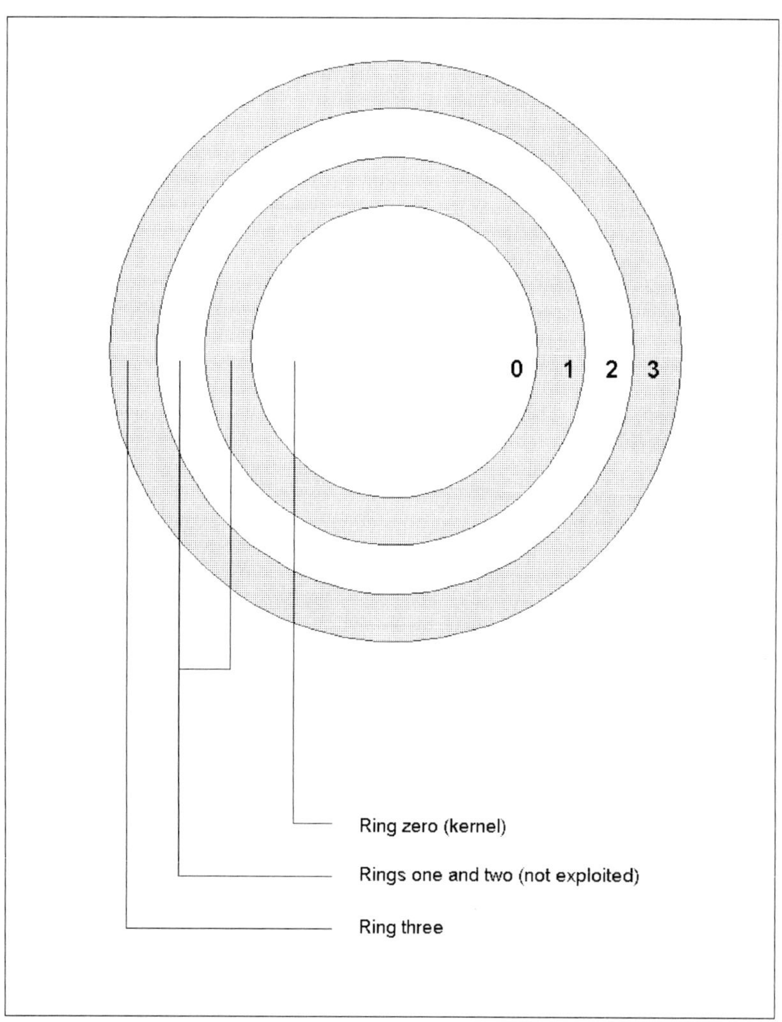

1. System architecture

Windows 95 has a modular design. It is made up of the following elements:

- the user interface,
- the core of Windows 95, which is itself composed of USER, GDI and KERNEL subsystems,
- the configuration registry
- the virtual machine manager,
- the manager for installable file systems,
- the configuration manager,
- virtual/real mode device drivers,

The different components fit together like this :

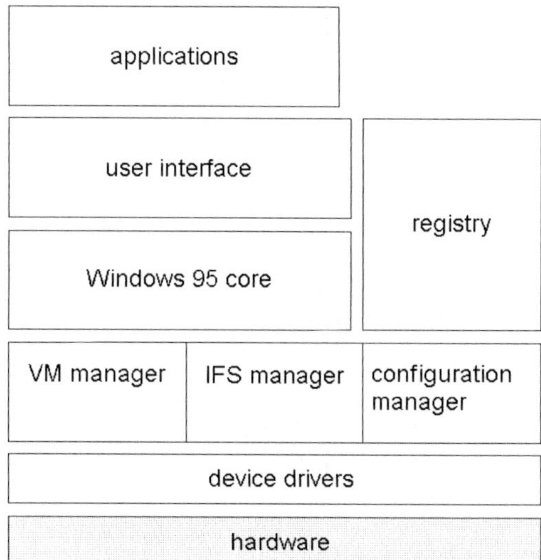

2. Virtual machines

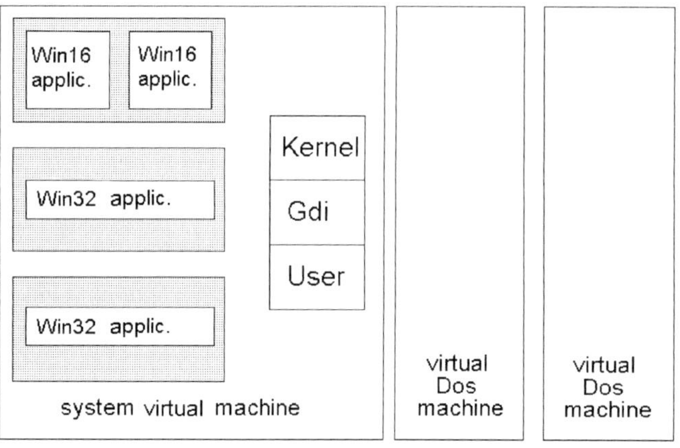

Windows 95's whole mode of functioning is based on the concept of virtual machines. A virtual machine is a complete environment recreated by the system to simulate a computer with all the resources (memory, devices) of a real physical machine.

The 80386 processor already had the capacity to simulate several 8086 processors. In Windows 95, an application runs inside a virtual machine running in ring three.

Only a small part of the system runs in ring zero: in particular, virtual device drivers or VXD and the elements of the system closest to the hardware.

The system exploits different types of virtual machine:
- the system virtual machine (SVM),
- virtual DOS machines.

The system virtual machine

This virtual machine corresponds to the core of Windows 95. All WIN32 or WIN16 applications function there.

It contains Windows' three principle subsystems (USER, GDI, KERNEL).

Each of these three subsystems exists in two versions, one 16-bit and one 32-bit.

KERNEL

It is implemented in the form of a dynamic link library. Its role is to carry out the basic functions of any operating system, such as:
– I/O execution,
– managing the memory (dynamic allocation),
– loading/unloading applications and running them,
– managing threads,
– synchronising processes,

GDI

The Graphic Device Interface is the basis of graphical functions in Windows, providing the basic elements for display and printing:
– the display of text graphics (TrueType manager),
– drawing, filling surfaces...,
– the printing subsystem and the spooler.
...

USER

USER32.DLL and USER.EXE make up the part of Windows which monitors user I/O operations, such as those carried out via the mouse or the keyboard.

This subsystem also manages sound and communication ports. The DLL handles management of windows and menus, as in earlier versions of Windows.
It is a complete asynchronous I/O subsystem.

16/32 bit call conversions are carried out using a technique called *thunking*.

32-bit Windows applications

Each application runs in a separate memory space inside the SVM. This ensures that a Windows 32-bit application which gets stuck cannot impede the running of the system or of another Windows 32-bit application. Each application's memory access is inaccessible to all other applications.

Each application also has its own queue of messages corresponding to events which have occurred. If a malfunctioning application does not read its messages, this will not prevent another application from consulting its own queue. This saves the system as a whole from locking up, as can happen with applications running under Windows 3.x.

Each 32-bit application has a virtual address space of 4 Gb.

16-bit Windows applications

They all run in the same memory space: this is to meet the requirement of compatibility with existing software. An errant 16-bit application is likely to cause all the other 16-bit applications to lock, and all the more so because all the 16-bit applications share the same message space. If one application stops reading the messages, the others are all held up.

Virtual DOS machines

Each MS-DOS application running under Windows 95 operates inside its own virtual DOS machine (VDM).

The virtual machine manager

The virtual machine manager is responsible for:
– scheduling processes,
– demand paging,
– supplying an MS-DOS protect mode interface.

Scheduling and the concept of threads

The experience of different designers of operating systems has been that creating and managing processes are operations which are costly for the system in terms of time. For any one process, a whole environment must be maintained, with various resources...

To limit the number of processes which need to be created, it is possible to divide a single process into several execution units, or *threads*. A 32-bit application can involve several threads, unlike MS-DOS and 16-bit Windows applications, which run as one threads. Threads can run at the same time, providing a kind of multitasking inside a single application.

Even though the various threads of a process can use the resources to which the process has access, ownership of the resources is retained by the process.

The scheduler allocates running time to the various threads pre-emptively: so that each gets a share of multiprocessing resources.

Priority of threads

There are thirty-two priority levels: 0 is the lowest and 31 the highest. Priorities above 15 correspond to real-time processes.

Dynamic modification of priority

The scheduler can decide to raise or lower the priority of a thread by two levels, to improve performance for the user or to regulate access to critical resources. It changes the priority dynamically.

Virtual memory

Address space

As mentioned above, each process which is running has available to it a virtual address space of 4 Gb divided into two sections. The upper two Gb are for the system and the lower two are for the application.

This virtual space is made up of pages, each of 4 Kb. These pages are exist either in the RAM or on the disk in a file known as a *paging file* or *swap file*. If the page required by a process is not in the RAM, the 80386 processor looks for the missing page in the swap file. In Windows 95, this file is called WIN386.SWP.

Configuring virtual memory

In Windows 95, the swap file is dynamic and the system can increase or reduce its size automatically. The user can decide to position the paging file on a different disk and can set upper and lower limits on its size:

☞ Double-click the My Computer icon

☞ Choose 

☞ Double-click System

☞ Open the **Performance** page.

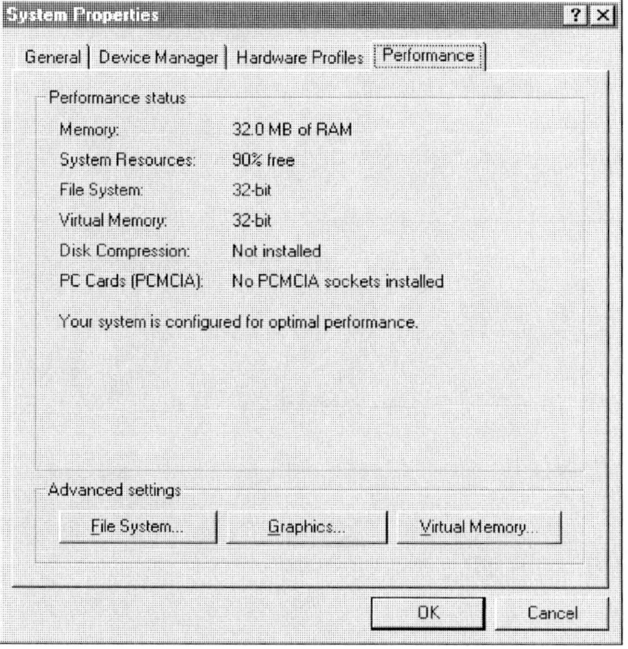

↓ personal notes ↓

☞ Click the **Virtual Memory** button.

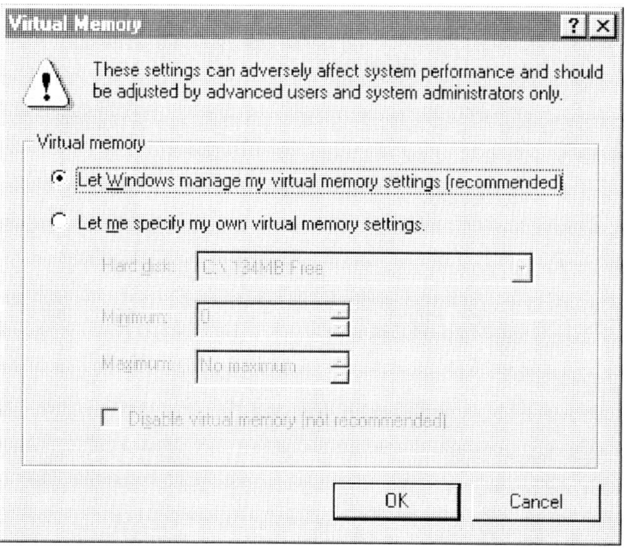

3. The IFS manager

Currently Windows 95 supports only two file systems: VFAT and CDFS. Future versions, however, may well be able to manage others, such as NTFS, if user demand or Microsoft policy requires it.

The Installable File System (IFS) manager governs access to the file system's resources.

It manages requests to the different file systems installed: local devices like VFAT or CDFS, or the network redirector, or the file system of another company (for example PC-NFS). This organisation gives applications a uniform view of the independent I/Os of the file system accessed:

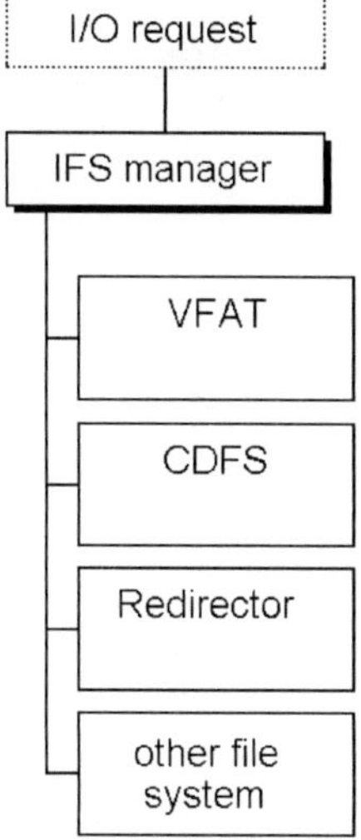

Long file names

In Windows 95, the VFAT is a 32-bit driver which manages long file names (LFN): a file name can be up to 255 characters long.

All new 32-bit applications have **Open** and **Save** dialog boxes which allow them to use long file names. Even at the DOS prompt, you can create a file with a long name, for example by redirecting: give the file name in quotation marks:

```
DIR > "really long file name"
```

↓ personal notes ↓

Disk / CD ROM cache

The IFS manager accesses the various file systems via a 32-bit cache driver, VCACHE which replaces SMARTDRIVE.exe. VCACHE manages a buffer whose size varies according to the amount of free system memory.

Optimising disk access

☞ Double-click 

☞ Choose 

☞ Double-click 

☞ Open the **Performance** page.

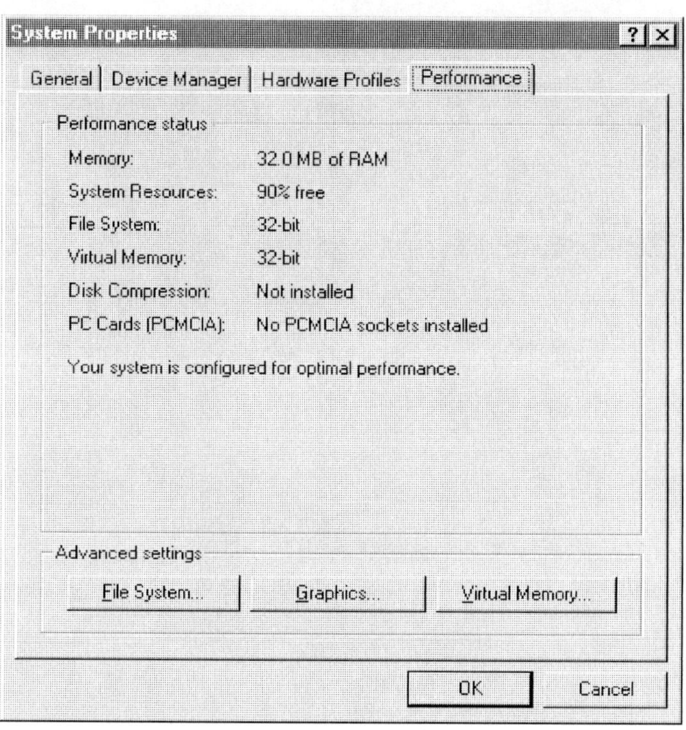

☞ Click the **File System** button.

☞ Open the **Hard Disk** page.

↓ personal notes ↓

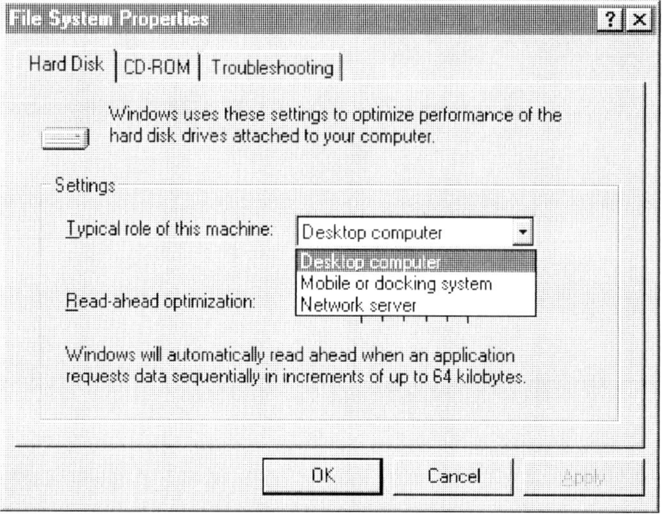

☞ Indicate the most common use of the computer and, taking into account the amount of free memory, set the parameters for the cache.
If the computer is equipped with a CD ROM drive, use the settings under the CD ROM tab to determine the size of the cache and the speed of access to the CD ROM drive:

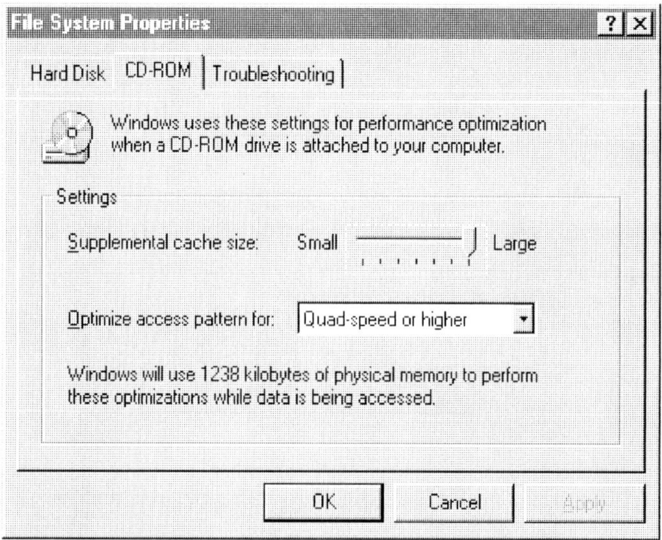

4. The configuration manager

The role of this new Windows component is to manage the *Plug and Play* functions of Windows 95. Its task is to identify the system buses and the devices connected to them then to ensure that each device has its I/O port or interruption vector, and that there are no conflicts. If the configuration changes dynamically - if for example a new PCMCIA device is added while the computer is running - the configuration manager is also responsible for informing the applications that the new device is available.

To resolve conflicts, the configuration manager may use various resource arbitrators. It lets the device drivers know which resources are available to them:

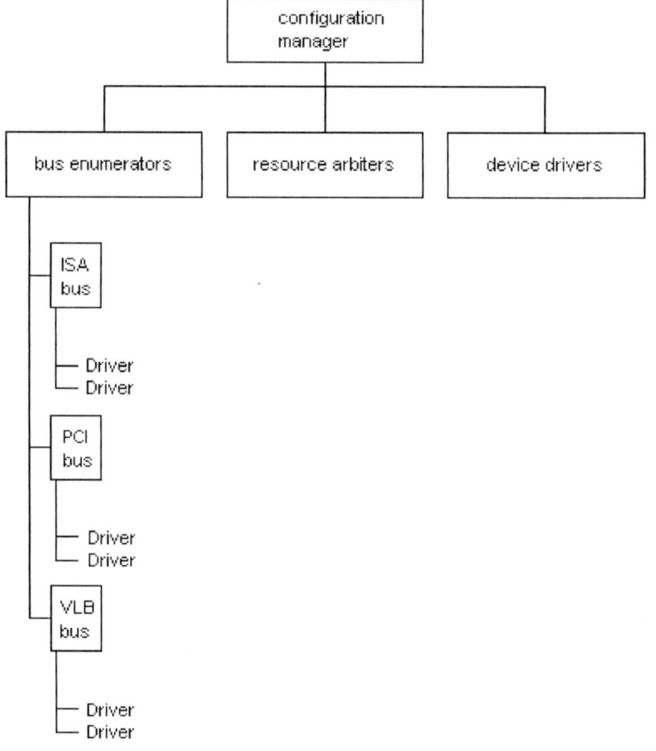

(see chapter 4 *The Plug and Play specification*).

↓ personal notes ↓

Installation

Installing Windows 95 is simple. It is even more simple if you are installing the system on a recent computer. Before you start, give some thought to the following points:

- Is the configuration of the machine where you want to install Windows 95 suited to the system ?
- Are you going to install Windows 95 from a CD ROM, a set of floppy disks... ?
- Is there a previous version of Windows on the machine, and do you want to conserve it ?
- If you are installing from a network server, do you want to perform a local installation or a shared one ?
- What type of installation (typical, custom...) do you require ?

The traditional *INSTALL* program recognises several command-line parameters:

Option	
/D	Do not base the installation on an existing version of Windows.
/I	Do not detect hardware.
/ID	Do not check the disk space.
Batch_name	Install from the script file which is named.
/?	Provide help with the INSTALL program.

A. Phases of the installation

There are four main phases to the installation:

- collecting the necessary information.
- copying files to the hard disk.
- restarting the computer.
- setting the remaining configuration parameters.

B. The required configuration

Hardware	Minimum required	Recommended
Processor	80386 SX	80486 dx2 66 or more
RAM	4 Mb	12 Mb
Hard disk	50 Mb	300 Mb or more
CD ROM drive	-	strongly recommended

C. Installing from a set of floppy disks or from a CD ROM

If the computer is not on a network, then installation is carried out from a set of disks or from a CD ROM. Currently, the version distributed on disks is different from the CD ROM version, which has additional elements. In particular, you can only perform a network installation from a CD ROM; The NETSETUP program is only available in the CD ROM version.

The Windows 95 installation files are compressed inside cabinet files which have the extension *.cab*. If, after installation you need to extract a file from one of the cabinets or to consult the contents, this is possible by means of the EXTRACT program.

Of course, during installation, the INSTALL program itself extracts the necessary files from the cabinets. This program is located in the \WIN95 directory on the CD ROM.

If your version of Windows 95 is an upgrade, you need to have a Windows 3.x version already installed on the computer before you can add Windows 95.

D. Upgrade or reinstallation

If you already have a version 3.x of Windows, you can choose between updating it, or installing Windows 95 separately in a different directory. Both choices have their advantages and disadvantages:

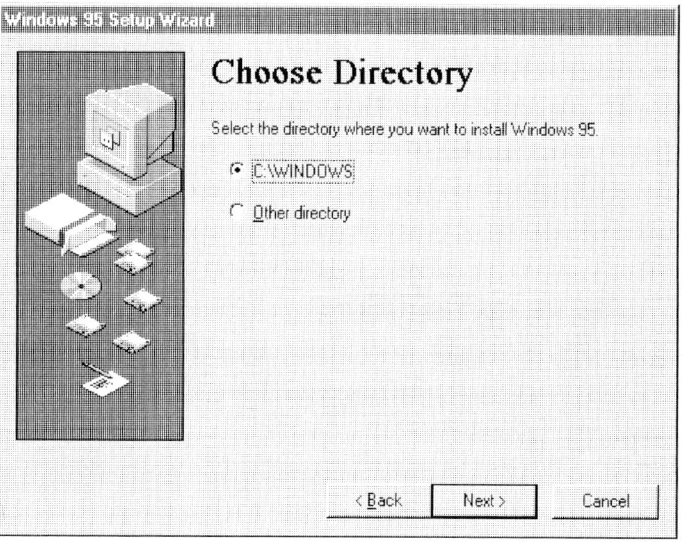

Installing in the same directory as the previous version conserves the parameters of your existing Windows installation, **in particular, the settings of the software installed**: Windows 95 uses the .INI files from the 16-bit version of Windows.

Even if the new applications designed for Windows 95 no longer need initialisation files, all the 16-bit Windows applications that you are going to continue using still need them.

Program groups too are automatically carried over into the new system.
The disadvantage of this method of installation is that it also conserves all the dynamic link library (DLL) files which are no longer in use, but which have accumulated in the WINDOWS directory over the years.

If you intend to reinstall your applications, or better still, to install the 32-bit versions, it is better to install Windows 95 from the ground up in a new directory.

Be careful to check that you have enough space on disk: when you install in a different directory to a previous Windows version, the two versions exist side by side at least for a short time. Once you have finished installing Windows 95, and have checked that no data file has accidentally been stored there, you can delete the old WINDOWS directory.

1. Type of installation

You have a choice of four different types of installation:

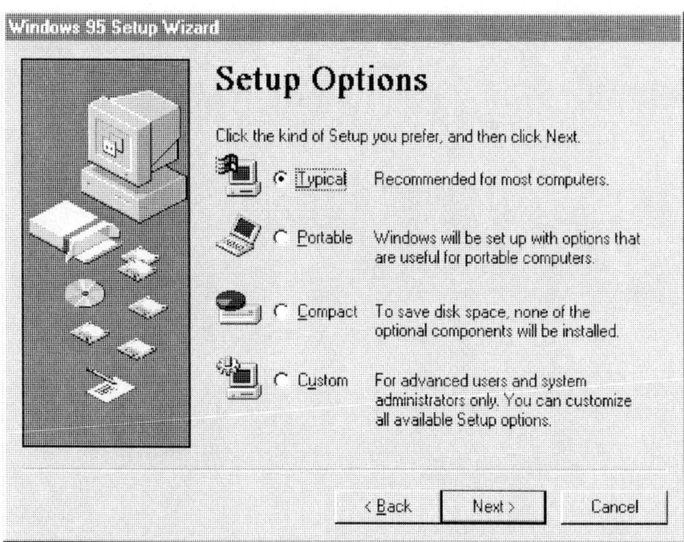

Only the custom installation allows you to decide all the parameters yourself. All the same, you should only really take this option if you are used to installing systems, Windows in particular.

Once you have chosen the type of installation, the next step is to identify the main user of the software, then to indicate whether or not you want to install connectivity options:

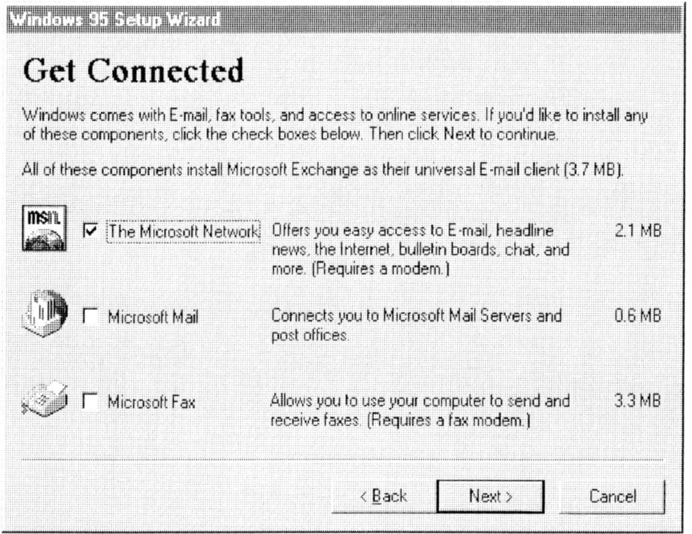

2. Choosing which components to install

At this point, you indicate whether you want to install the set of standard components or if you want to choose exactly which components you need:

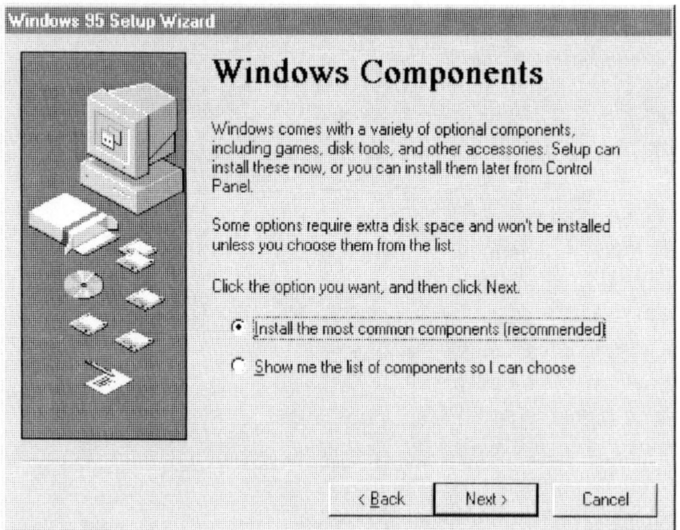

Whether you are performing a typical installation or a custom one, you have the opportunity of choosing which components to install. Whatever you choose at this stage, you can always add or remove components once the installation is complete.

For details of adding an element to the system or removing one, see chapter 3 *Changing the configuration.*

3. Creating a boot disk

The system prompts you to create a system floppy, and it is advisable to create one. The files on a Windows 95 system disk are not identical to those on an MS-DOS boot disk. The files on the disk are as follows:

File	Size	**Role**
command.com	94822	command interpreter
io.sys		boot file equivalent to the DOS' io.sys + msdos.sys
msdos.sys		editable text file containing startup options
drvspace.bin	71431	disk compression driver
format.com	41175	format command
sys.com	13479	system transfer command
config.sys		the same as it always has been
autoexec.bat		also unchanged
edit.com	71086	text editor (no longer needs qbasic.exe)
regedit.exe	123904	configuration registry editor
scandisk.exe	137744	command for scanning and repairing disks
scandisk.ini	7675	settings for scandisk.exe
fdisk.exe	60280	command for partitioning a disk
keyb.com	20135	international keyboard driver program
Keyboard.sys	34566	international keyboard driver
attrib.exe	15348	command which manages file attributes
debug.exe	21146	debugging tools/assembler
chkdsk.exe	27904	command for repairing disks
mode.com	29831	management of console internationalisation
display.sys	17239	manages display of international characters
country.sys	27094	internationalisation driver (date/time/numbers...)
uninstal.exe	76704	program for removing Windows 95

It is possible to recreate this boot disk at a later date (see chapter 11 *Troubleshooting*, the section on *Creating a boot disk*).

4. Restarting the computer

When the system has finished creating the boot disk, it informs you that it is going to restart the computer to finish the installation:

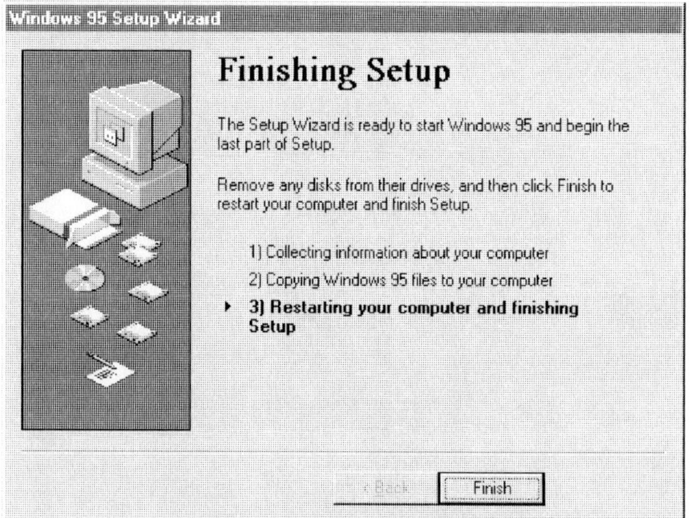

5. Final phase

Once the computer has restarted, there are still a certain number of tasks to perform:

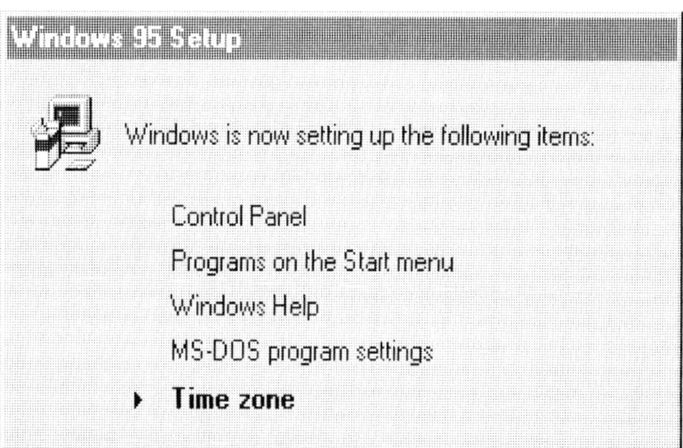

These tasks are taken care of automatically by Windows, but it does need you to specify which time zone you are in:

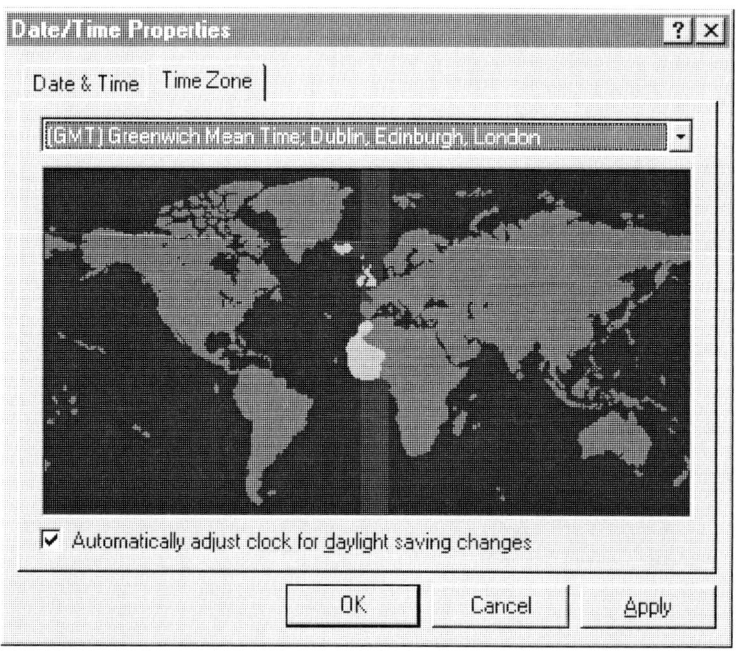

Windows might also need you to tell it whether or not to add a printer or a modem.

This is the end of the installation, the window illustrated below appears: use it to go through the on line registration procedure if you have a modem, or to view a presentation of Windows 95 or to discover the new features of this version:

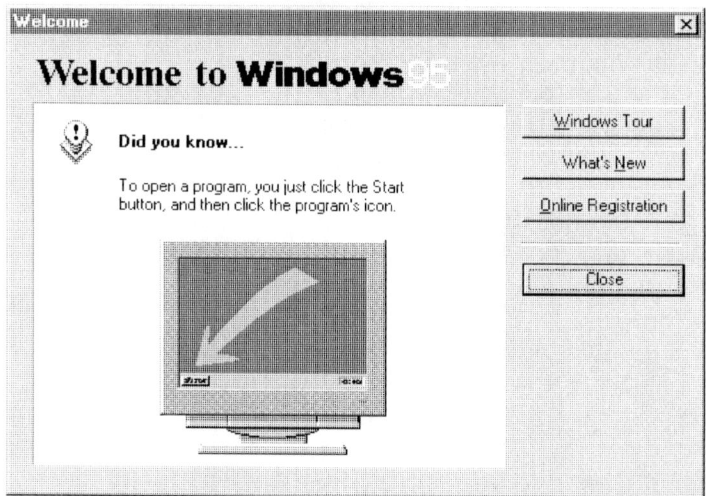

E. Installing from a network server

If you have a network server to which the intended Windows 95 workstations can connect, you will certainly prefer to install the system on the workstations from the server. Not only does this save you from having to handle disks or a CD ROM, but it greatly increases the speed of the installation.

There are two stages to a network installation:
- administrative installation of all the Windows 95 files onto the server,
- connection of the workstation to the server and local or shared installation of Windows 95.

1. Administrative installation

The first operation, the administrative installation, already existed with earlier versions of Windows, by means of the option /A. In Windows 95, that option has disappeared and has been replaced by a specialised program: NETSETUP.EXE.

Here are two important points to bear in mind:
- Copying files *onto* the server, and consequently running NETSETUP.EXE, can only be carried out *correctly* from a Windows 95 machine. There must *imperatively* be at least one workstation where Windows 95 is already installed.
- The program NETSETUP.EXE *only* exists on the CD ROM version of Windows 95. It is located in the directory *\ADMIN\NETTOOLS\NETSETUP*.

The person who carries out the installation will need to write in a shared resource on the server: he/she must have the necessary permissions with regard to the resource. In general, the system administrator carries out the installation. The server from which Windows 95 is installed can be:
- an NT Server machine,
- a Novell server,
- another Windows 95 machine,
- a Windows for Workgroups machine,
- in fact, any NetBIOS server....

☞ Run the NETSETUP.EXE program:

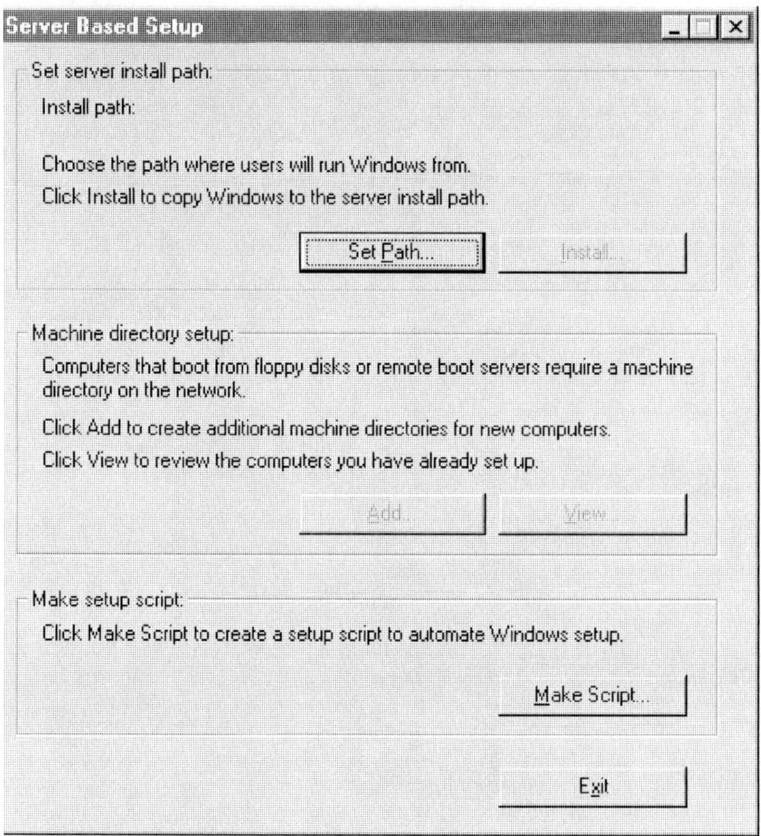

☞ Click the **Seth Path** button.

This dialog box allows you to define the location to which the Windows 95 files are copied, that is, the location from which the workstations will later be installed. This location must be given as a UNC (Universal Naming Convention) name and must correspond to a valid shared resource on the server:

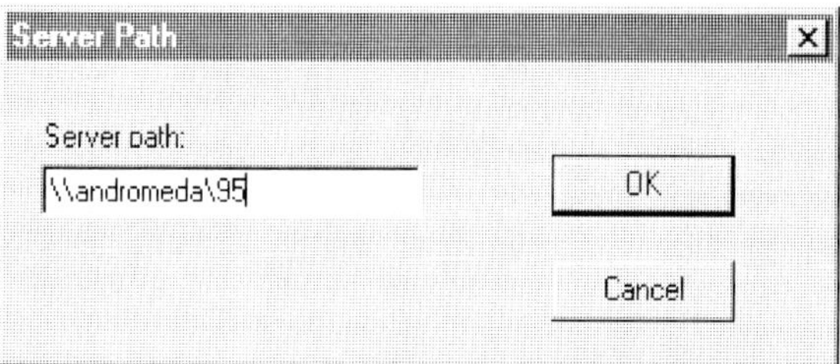

☞ Click **OK**.

The **Install** button becomes available: click it to continue the installation. The following screen appears:

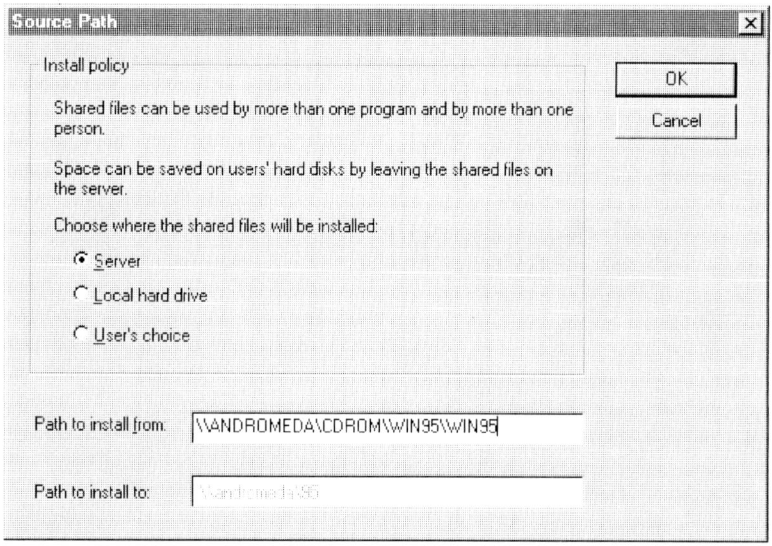

At this point, you need to indicate how you intend to install the workstations later on. There are three possibilities:

- installing in shared mode: the files, for the most part, exist only on the server,
- installing a complete version of Windows 95 on each the hard disk of each workstation (standard installation),
- choosing one or other of the above options for each workstation individually: you indicate which at the start of the installation procedure.

This is the only information that you need to give at this stage.
The source path is automatically correct: it is the location of the Windows 95 CD ROM, that is, where you found the NETSETUP.EXE file. The CD ROM might be local (the path looks something like D:\WIN95) or it could even be a CD ROM shared on the server.

The destination path is correct: it is the path you gave earlier.

☞ Click **OK** to confirm.

Default installation options

The next step is to decide whether or not you wish to set default values for installation parameters:

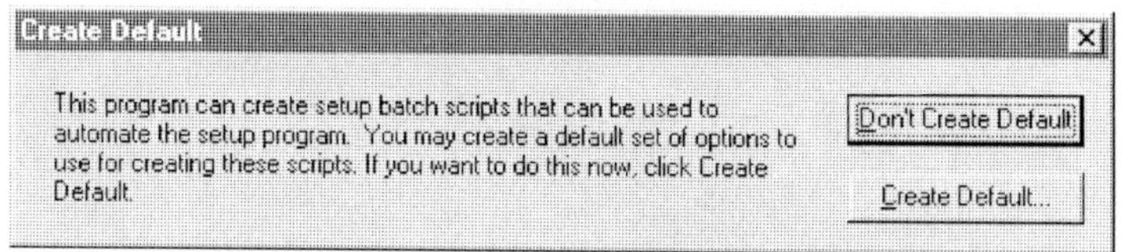

Creating the default options can save you having to supply a certain amount of repetitive information for each workstation you install. The options are stored in a file named MSBATCH.INF.

☞ To set an installation parameter, activate its check box and give the default value:

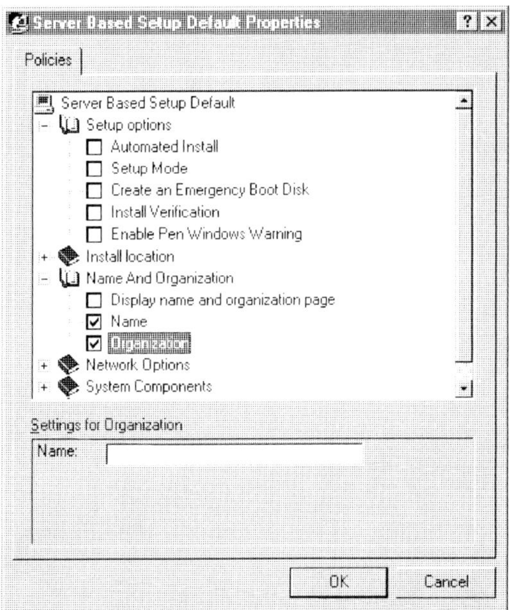

☞ Once the options have been set, click **OK** and enter the product identification number:

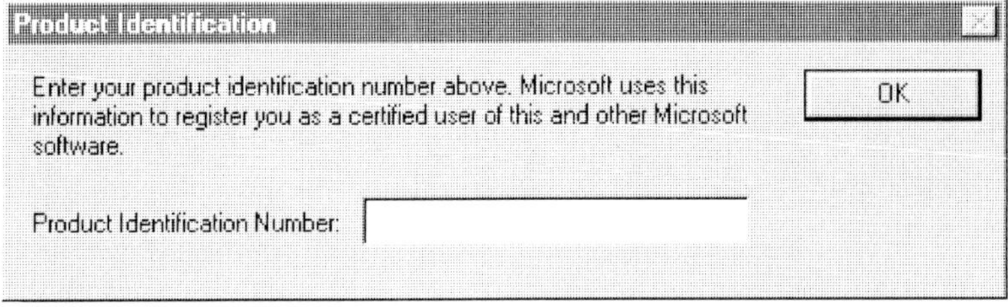

The program starts to copy the files onto the server:

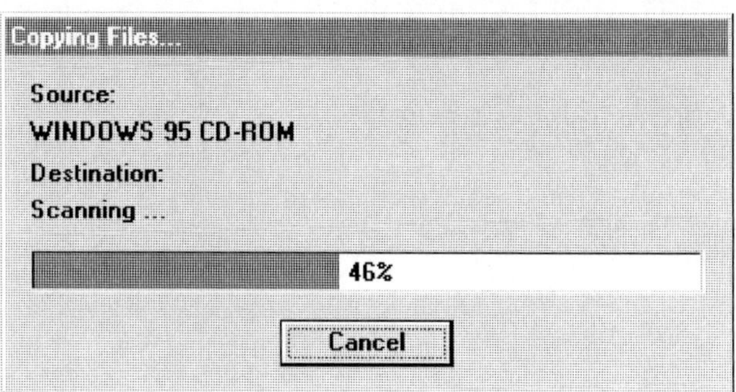

At the end of this operation, the administrative installation is complete.

You can, at this point, create one or more installation scripts to automate the installation of the workstations (see the section on *Automated installation* later on in the chapter).

2. Installing a workstation from the server

Now that the server is installed, you can go on to install Windows 95 on the workstations. Of course, for this, the workstations must already be able to access the server and its resource which contains the Windows 95 installation files !

The connection can be made by means of one of the three following clients:

- Microsoft MS-DOS 3.0 client.
  This software is included on the NT Server CD ROM, it takes up just one or two diskettes and is ideal for accessing the server. You should use the NetBEUI protocol which comes with this client (TCP/IP does not... !).

- LANManager 2.x client
  This client is rather older and takes up more space than the 3.0 client, but it does the same job.
- Windows for Workgroups
  If you already have this client, there will be no problem connecting to the installation server.

Apart from the connection to the server's shared resource (the NET USE command or the file manager) the installation goes ahead like any other: use the INSTALL command to start it.

3. Local or shared installation

If you have already carried out an administrative installation on a network server, you have two options for installing the workstations:

- Local installation.
  All the Windows 95 files are copied onto the workstation.

Advantages	Disadvantages
The workstation runs independently	even if the server is not operational.
	Updating Windows 95 takes longer.

- Shared installation (workstation).
  Only a small part of the files which make up Windows 95 are copied onto the workstation: the rest are accessible on the server.

Advantages	Disadvantages
This type of installation takes up little space on the workstation.	Windows loads more slowly.
Updating Windows 95 takes less time.	It creates a lot of traffic on the network.
Security is optimised.	

4. Automated installation

You can automate the installation of Windows 95 by supplying, as a parameter of the INSTALL command, the name of an information file with the extension .INF. This file contains the procedure to follow for setting the installation options.

By default, this file is MSBATCH.INF. If you want to create your own .INF file, you can use one of three methods:

Use a text editor to create the file on your own.

Use the option in NetSetup which enables you to create installation scripts

Use the BATCH.EXE program situated in the \ADMIN\NETTOOLS\NETSETUP directory on the CD ROM which creates scripts (even if you are not installing in a network).

This last program supplies the most comprehensive help: notably, it provides an easy way of indicating which components to install.

5. Detecting the configuration

During its installation, Windows 95 detects all the devices installed. In general, this gives entirely satisfactory results.

All the same, some components, especially the older ones, cannot be detected without risk of system failure. If the hardware does not support detection (*Plug and Play*), Windows 95 uses aggressive detection techniques, testing the various device drivers in the I/O addresses.

Windows 95 keeps three log files:

- C:\DETLOG.TXT
  logs the cards and hardware components detected.
- C:\SETUPLOG.TXT
  contains installation information which is valuable when events occur during the detection phase of the installation.
- C:\DETCRASH.LOG
  a binary file which is created if the system fails during the detection and the startup which follows it.

If a problem occurs, Windows 95 can use these last two files to pinpoint it and skip the detection operation which caused it. This means that Windows proceeds with the installation rather than getting stuck again at the same point.

The ability to do this is particularly valuable at the present moment, when the transition to Plug and Play technology is not yet complete and not all machine configurations support it.

Changing the configuration

↓ personal notes ↓

A. Changing the local configuration

One of the problems experienced with the versions 3.x of Windows was the difficulty of removing programs once they were installed. With Windows 95 applications, the difficulty no longer exists: any new 32-bit application designed for Windows 95 can be uninstalled, entirely or partially. The new 32-bit applications no longer use .INI files: they store their configuration data in a hierarchical tree, in the configuration registry.

To add Windows 95 components or to remove them, the route is the same.

1. Adding or removing programmes included in Windows 95

To add a new program, or to remove an existing one:

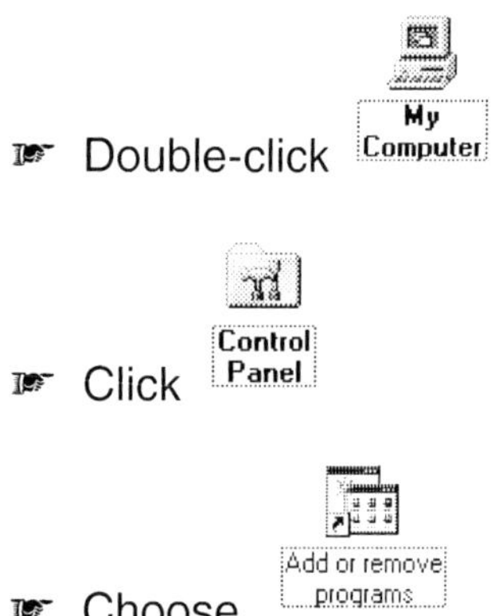

☞ Activate the **Windows Setup** tab.

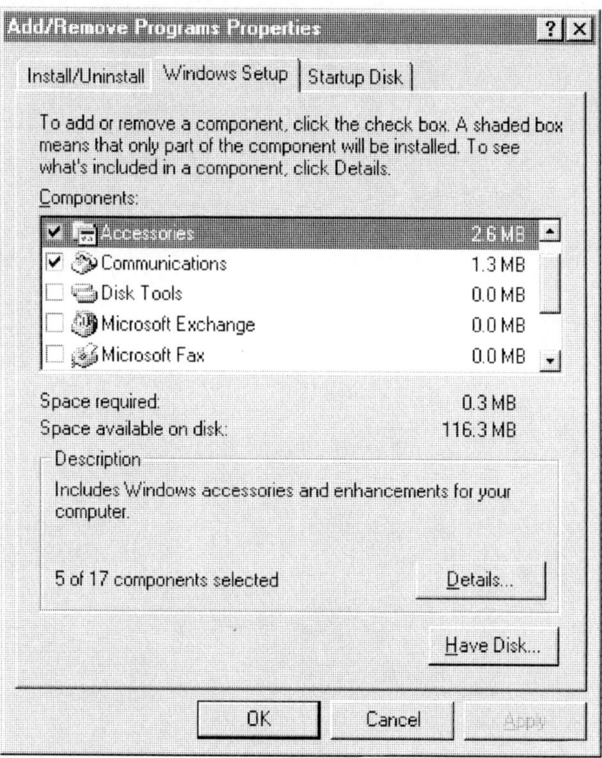

For each category of program (**Accessories, Communications**...), this window tells you whether the category is installed entirely (white box with check mark), partially (shaded box with check mark) or not at all (empty box).

↓ personal notes ↓

The **Details** button gives you access to a set of components in each category. Activate or clear the check box by a component to add or remove it:

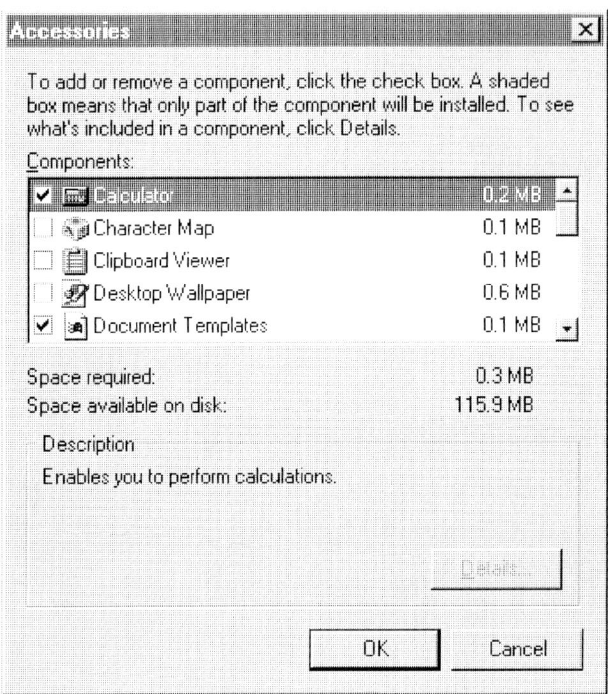

2. Adding or removing applications

To modify one of the logical components of an application or to uninstall it, completely or partially:

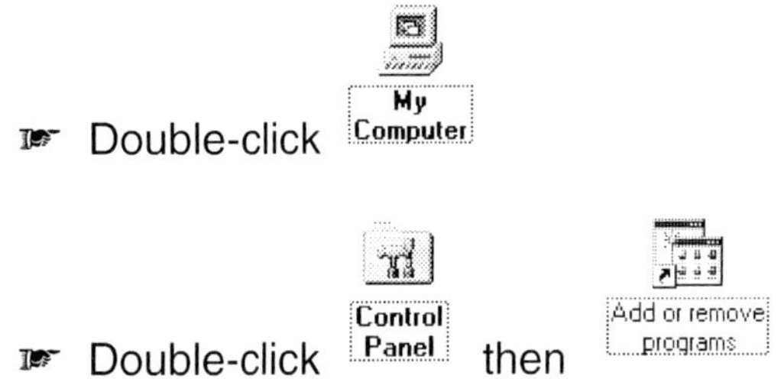

☞ Double-click My Computer

☞ Double-click Control Panel then Add or remove programs

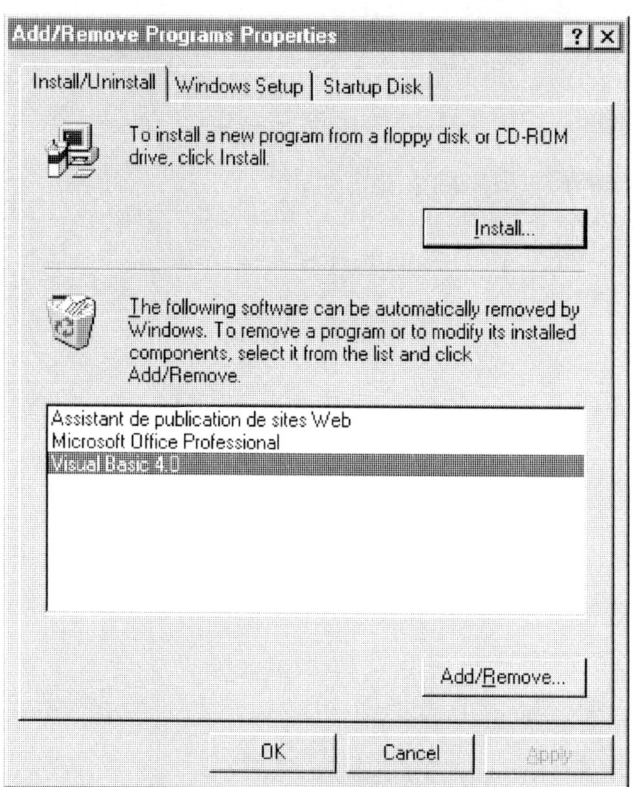

The **Install/Uninstall** tab, you can select the application that you wish to remove entirely or partially. Only applications which have been designed for Windows 95 appear in this window. Older 16-bit applications continue to use WIN.INI and SYSTEM.INI (which continue to exist just for this purpose).

B. Changing the hardware configuration

1. Adding a device

A new device can be added either by allowing the system to detect it automatically or by specifying exactly which device you are installing.

To install a new device:

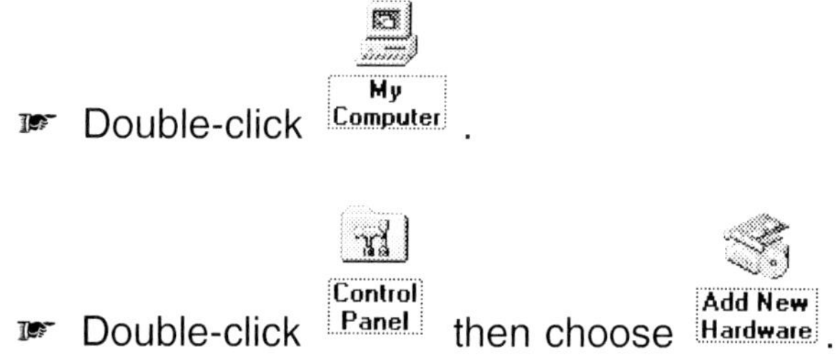

☞ Double-click My Computer.

☞ Double-click Control Panel then choose Add New Hardware.

The **Add New Hardware Wizard** starts:

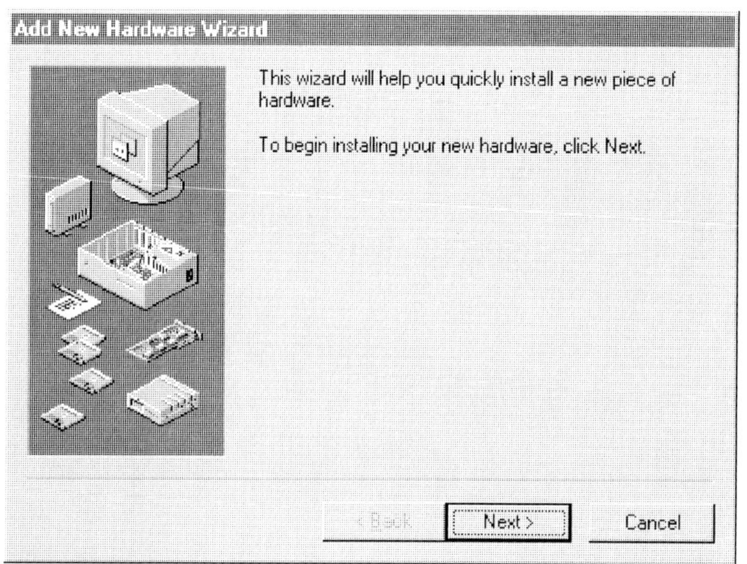

☞ Click the **Next** button.

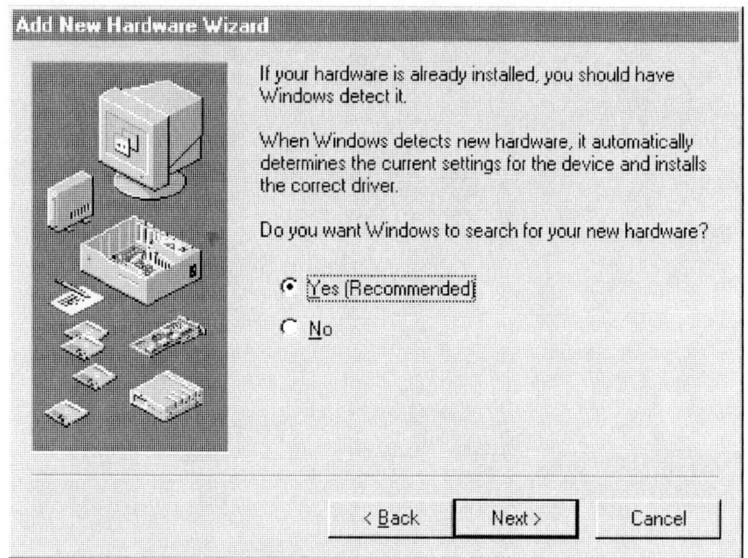

The first thing you need to tell the system is whether you want Windows 95 to detect the new device(s), or whether you are going to supply the information about them yourself.

☞ Click the **Next** button to start the detection process. This can take several minutes.

Windows 95 displays the usual warning messages:

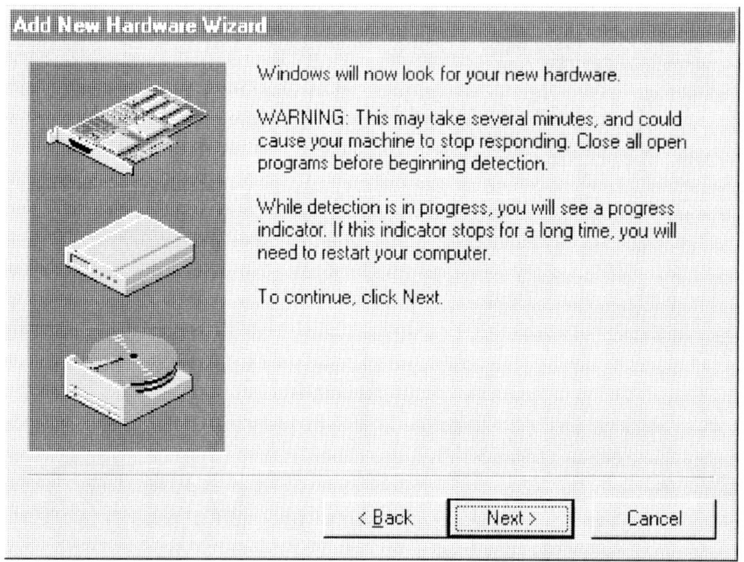

When the detection has been completed, you can see which hardware has been detected by clicking the **Details** button:

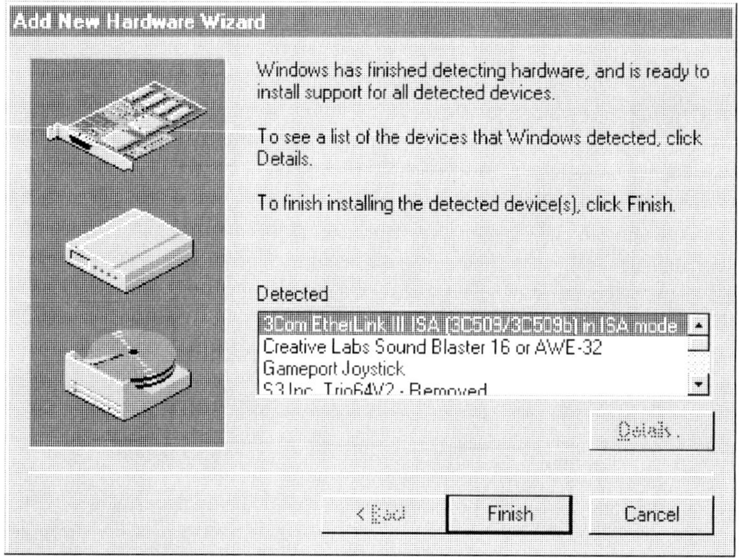

- If you are satisfied with the results of the detection, click the **Finish** button and go on to copy the required device drivers from the installation source (resource on a server, CD ROM or floppy disks).

The new device appears in the system property sheet. To display this window:

- Double-click My Computer followed by Control Panel then System.
- Click the **Device Manager** tab.

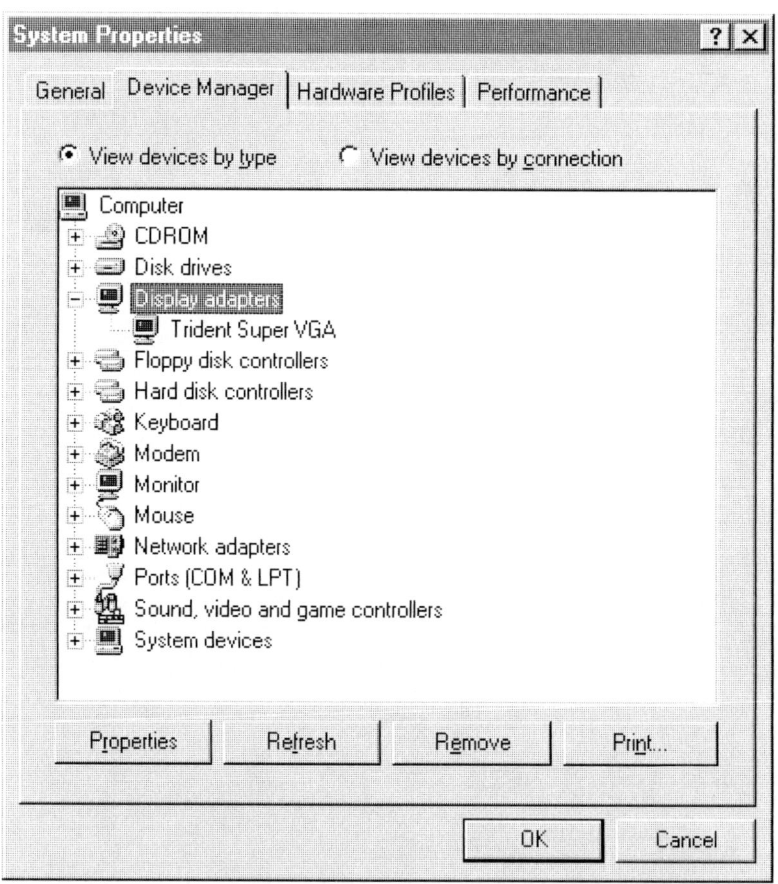

Click the **+** sign by a category to see which devices in the category are installed.

In cases where a device is faulty, is involved in a interruption conflict... this is the dialog box where you can pinpoint the problem and solve it. An icon which represents a problematic device is marked with a black exclamation mark on a yellow background.

☞ For further information on a device, click the **Properties** button. On the **General** page, you can check the status of the device.

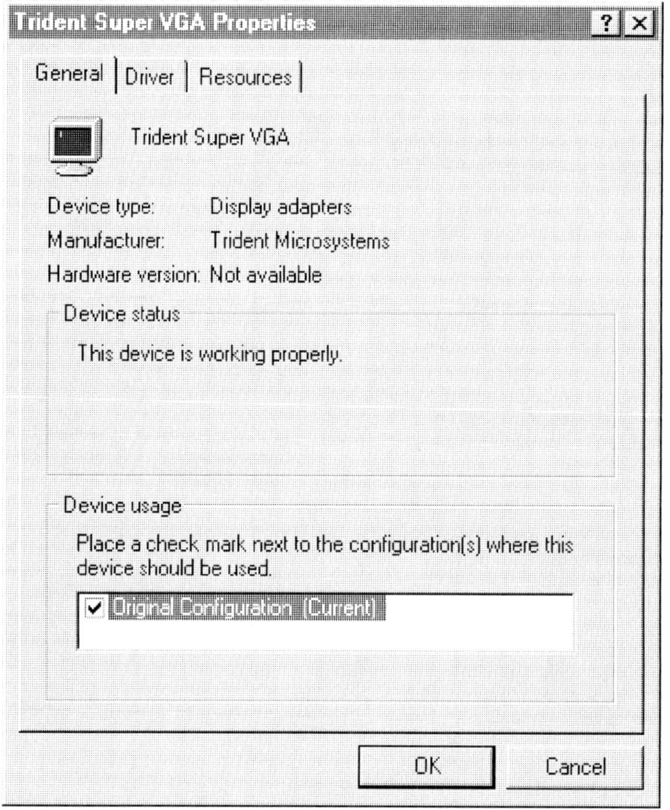

The **Driver** page displays the list of files which make up the device's driver and, more importantly, its version :

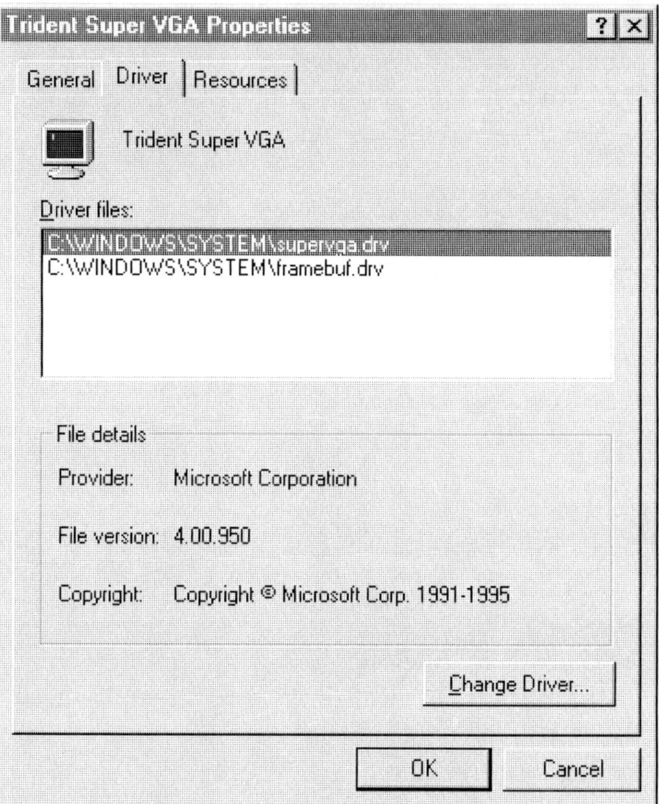

The **Resources** page supplies two sets of information: the current status of the I/O ports and interrupts, and details of any conflicts. It also provides the means of changing the resource parameters.

2. Changing the configuration of a device

It is possible to modify manually the interruption of a device or the address of its I/O port. This is a delicate operation which should only be performed in exceptional circumstances, since an error could cause the computer to go down. Even if you are sure of what you are doing, you should use a greater than usual degree of caution !

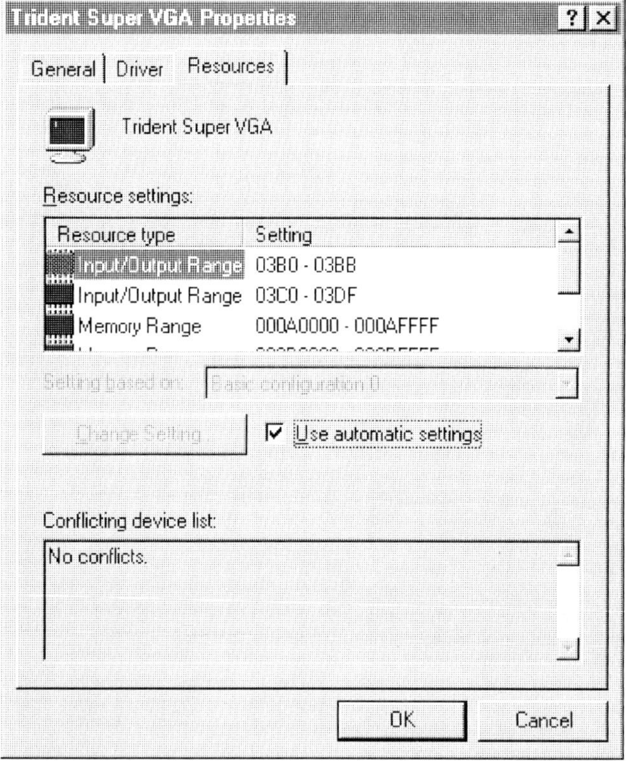

To change one of the settings:

☞ On the **Resources** page, deactivate the **Use automatic settings** option.

☞ Select the parameter concerned.

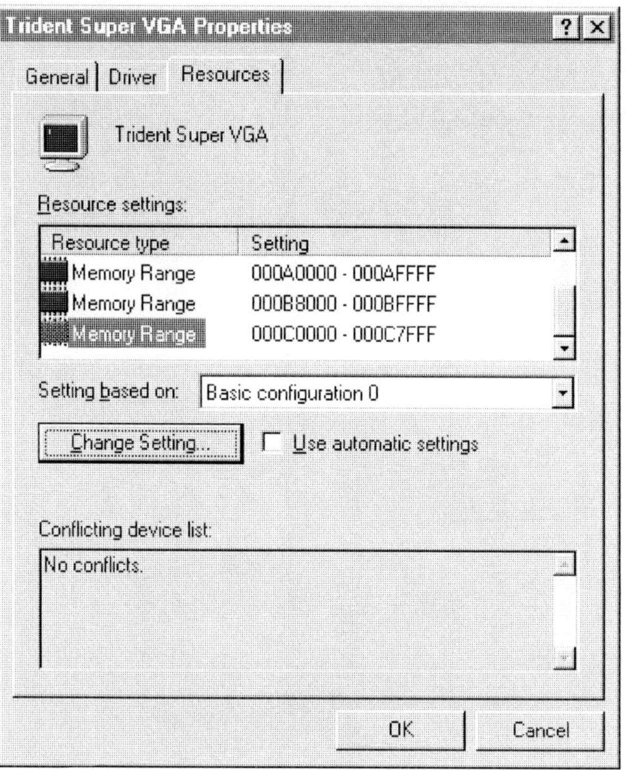

☞ Click the **Change Setting** button.

☞ Give the new value.

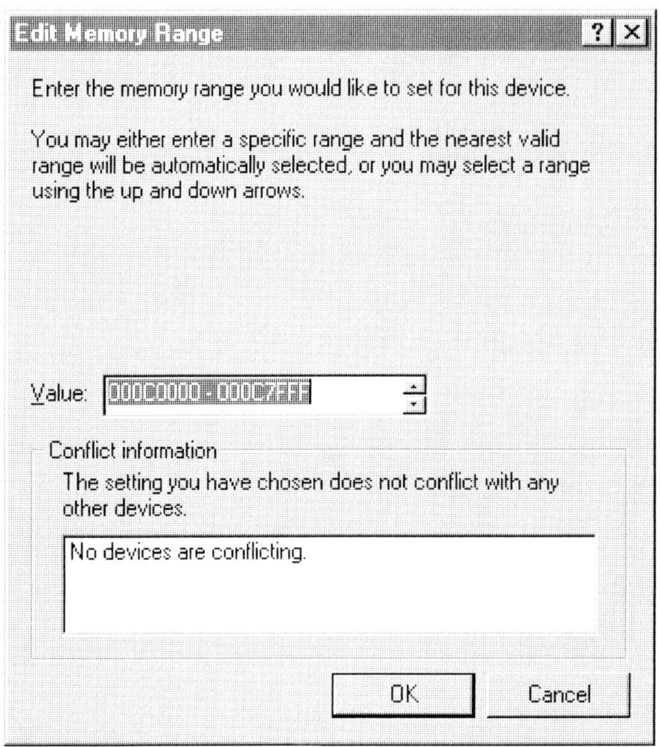

☞ Click **OK** to confirm.

3. Removing a device

This to is a risky operation which should only be underta-ken if absolutely necessary and by an expert.

To delete a device:

☞ Double-click  .

☞ Activate the **Device Manager** tab.

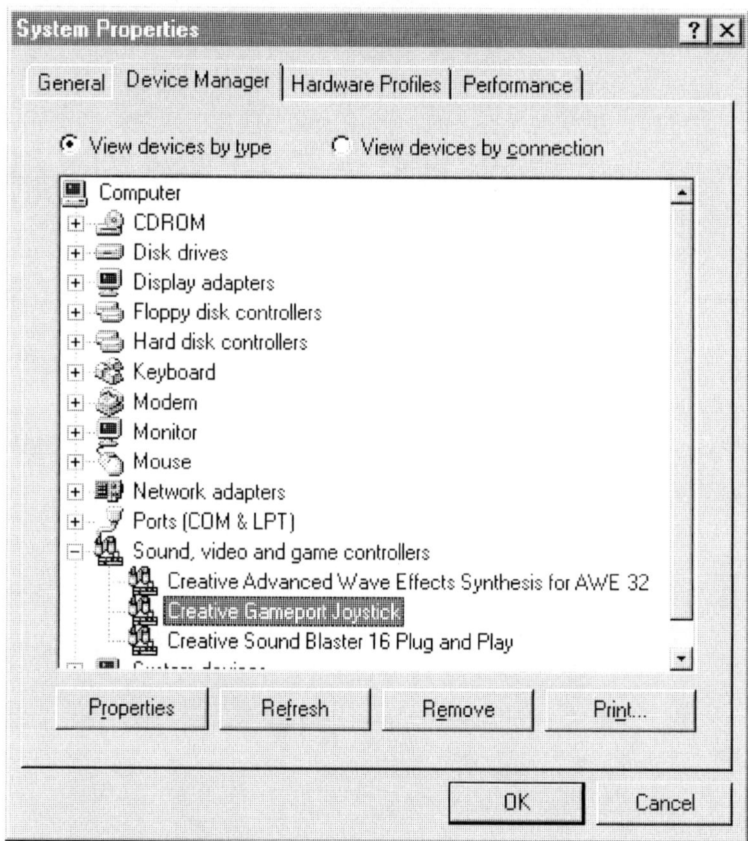

☞ Select the device in question and click the **Remove** button.

☞ Click **OK** to validate the deletion.

↓ personal notes ↓

The Plug and Play specification

One of the new features fundamental to Windows 95 is its *Plug and Play* (*PnP*) capacity. This permits you to plug in any compatible device and start working with it straight away, without having to go through any kind of configuration procedure.

Plug and Play goes even further: a device does not even need to be plugged in (connected via a bus or a cable): Windows 95 is, in theory, able to detect and use any infrared device in a given perimeter.

When you consider the current rush to produce this type of device, particularly in conjunction with network technology, you can imagine the revolution that this is set to provoke. A few years from now, configuring, and even plugging in, devices will be no more than a memory.

Bearing in mind the great variety of devices which Windows 95 recognises, this technology seems all the more impressive, even if the detection of devices will not be perfect until all manufacturers have adopted the PCI bus, the only one to offer real PnP capacities.

A. Aims of the Plug and Play specification

- A Plug and Play system should make it possible to add or remove new devices in a way which is completely dynamic, without it being necessary to restart the computer.
- Devices added in this way must be exploitable without any manual configuration.

1. Auto-identification of devices

The Plug and Playspecification states that all new devices designed as Plug and Play should be able to auto-identify themselves and to inform the system of all their capacities. For example, a Plug and Play video adapter must indicate to the system all the resolutions/palettes it has available.

2. Adding/removing dynamic devices

It must be possible to establish any connection, physical or infrared, without having to restart the computer. For the time being, only PC cards with the PCMCIA format can be connected without restarting the computer.

Windows 95 supports three types of connection:

- the device can be connected while the computer is running (*Hot swapping*).
- the device can be connected while the computer is in suspend mode.
- the device can be connected while the computer is switched off.

Docking, connecting a portable computer to a docking station, is a good example of a connection which it is desirable to make while the computer is running *(Hot docking)*.

3. Upward compatibility

New devices should be compatible with the specification, but what about the older (*legacy*) ones ? Windows 95 can use an "aggressive" detection technique to detect a legacy device.

This "aggressive" detection involves loading all possible drivers for the category of device into the memory (for instance, all the network adapter drivers) until one is found to fit. This function is, of course, only a stop-gap, useful until all devices can auto-identify themselves and Plug and Play detection becomes totally reliable. If Windows has no way of detecting the hardware, the user is asked to supply the necessary information.

B. Elements of a Plug and Play system

A true Plug and Play system is made up of three elements:

– a PnP BIOS,

– a PnP operating system,

– PnP devices and drivers.

If one of these three components is missing, another can stand in for it, at least partially.

1. The BIOS

The BIOS itself should be able to detect and identify internal devices and should be capable of informing the system of any change in configuration (*docking or other*). The BIOS only has PnP capacities on relatively recent machines, those with Pentium processors, for example.

Windows 95 can often compensate for a lack of PnP BIOS by searching out the information that the BIOS has not supplied.

2. The operating system

To provide PnP functions, Windows 95 includes the following elements:

A configuration manager

This part of the software is responsible for the hardware configuration. It maintains a dialogue with all the elements involved in the procedure (arbitrators, components...). In particular, it prompts the resource arbiters to allocate resources, either at system startup, or when it has notice of the dynamic introduction of a new device, that is, a new call on resources.

Bus device lists

There are programs capable of collecting and passing on to the configuration manager the list of the devices connected to a particular bus.

Bus	List file
PCI	PCI.VXD
EISA	EISA.VXD
ISA PnP	ISAPNP.VXD
SCSI	SCSI driver
PCMCIA	card drivers

Notice that there are no list files for MCA and VLB...

Resource arbitrators

These programs allocate resources to various devices and manage conflicts. The types of resource involved are:
- interrupts,
- DMA channels,
- I/O memory addresses,
- I/O port addresses.

Details of the allocation of resources are stored in the registry (the configuration database).

Example of a hierarchical system for storing the hardware configuration: this storage system is a tree structure in the memory, under HKEY_LOCAL_MACHINE in Windows 95's configuration registry. It is stored in a file named SYSTEM.DAT:

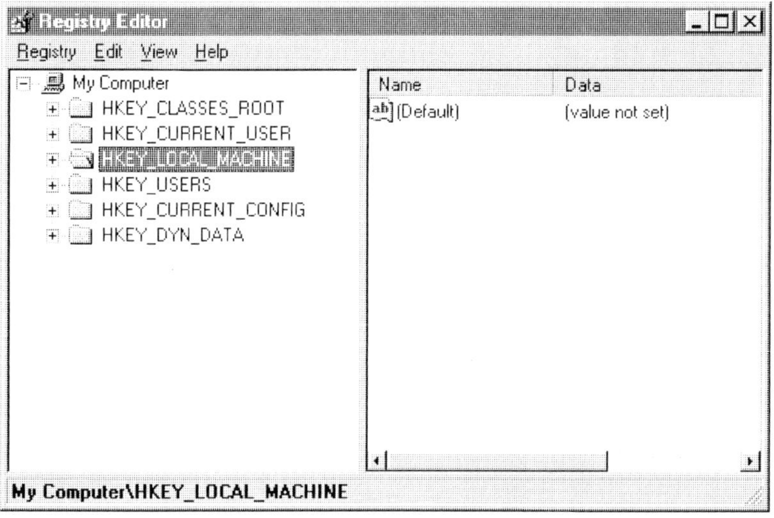

This hierarchy is recreated each time you start Windows 95 and is updated dynamically.

3. Devices and drivers

To meet the TCP/IP specification, device drivers must be dynamic: it must be possible to load and unload them at will. They must be capable of sustaining a dialog with the configuration manager and they must remain inactive during resource arbitration. They must also inform applications which are running if a dynamic reconfiguration of the computer takes place, letting them know, for example, if a device is added or removed.

↓ personal notes ↓

MS-DOS Applications

The task of designing a new operating system would have been much simpler if it had been possible to impose the exclusive use of new applications custom-built for the system. This, of course, was a luxury denied to the designers of Windows 95, whose brief was to ensure that existing MS-DOS applications would work perfectly under the new system.

The user of a DOS application under Windows 95 has access to a wide range of choices concerning the behaviour and appearance of the DOS program. As described in this chapter, all the elements of the PIF files used by earlier versions of Windows are still available.

A. The property sheet of a DOS application

In the Explorer window, a right-click on the name of a program allows you to display its property sheet. The properties are grouped together into different categories, each under its individual tab:
General, Program, Font, Memory, Screen, Miscellaneous.

1. General properties

On this page, you can set the attributes of a file, executable or not. These properties are common to all Windows or MS-DOS applications:

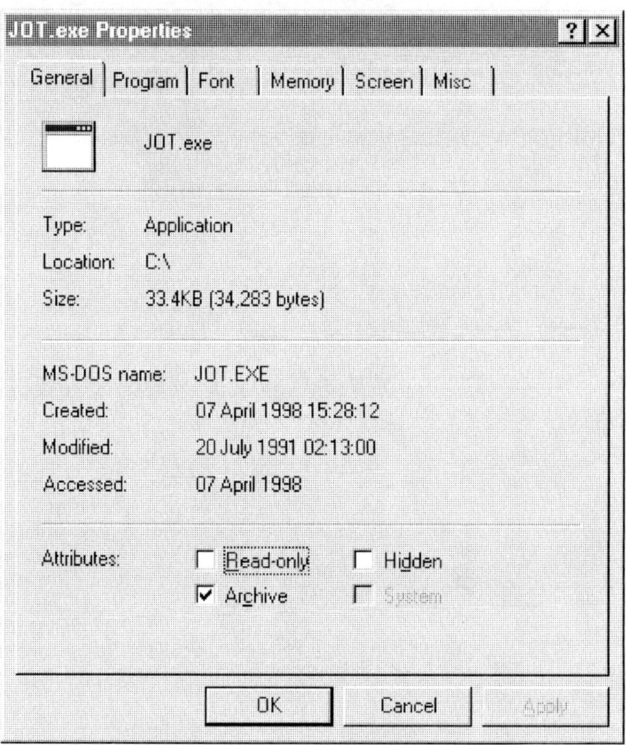

2. Program properties

On this page, you define:

- the working directory,
- the corresponding shortcut key,
- the path to any batch file which may run *before* an application starts, to load a resident program,
- the appearance of the application (icon, window or maximised),
- whether or not the window should close when you leave the application,
- the icon which represents the application.

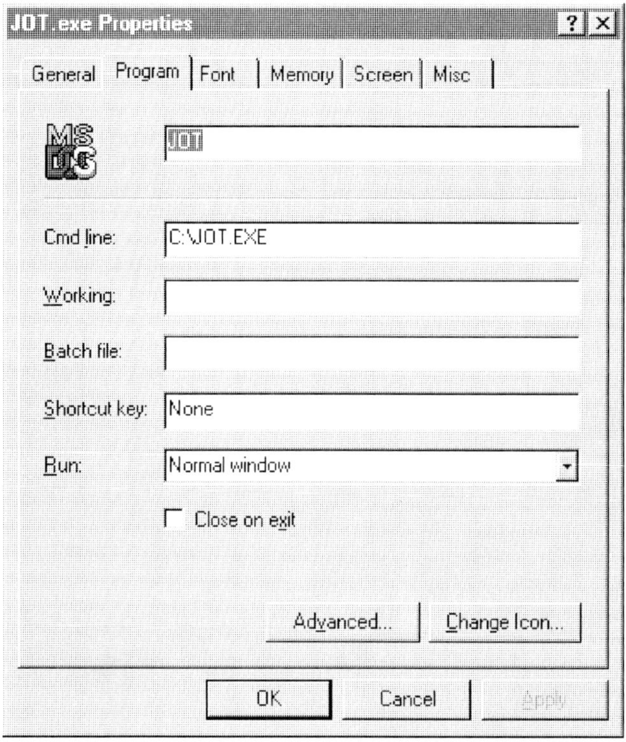

By adjusting the program properties of an application, you create a file with the extension .PIF and the same name as the application.

The **Advanced** button is important: it provides the possibility of creating a specific AUTOEXEC.BAT or CONFIG.SYS for an application:

☞ Activate the **MS-DOS mode** check box and enter the new MS-DOS configuration:

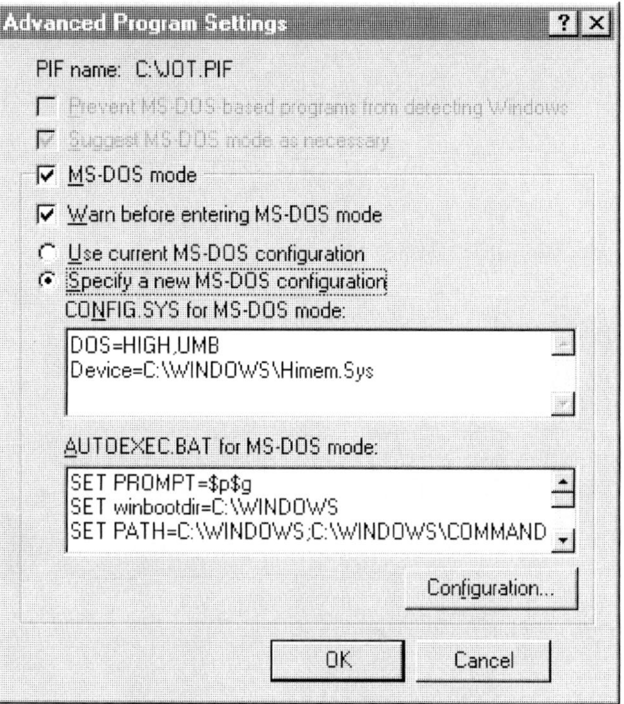

If you choose the option **Use current MS-DOS configuration**, the standard AUTOEXEC.BAT and CONFIG.SYS files (located at c:\) are used.

If you specifically indicate that MS-DOS mode should be used, as opposed to letting Windows 95 find the appropriate DOS mode for you, starting the application will cause the computer to restart in MS-DOS mode. Because of this, the option should only be used as a last resort, when there is no other way to make the option run correctly.

↓personal notes↓

3. Font properties

These properties are available for applications which do not need to restart in MS-DOS mode. They set the font used in the application window and its size:

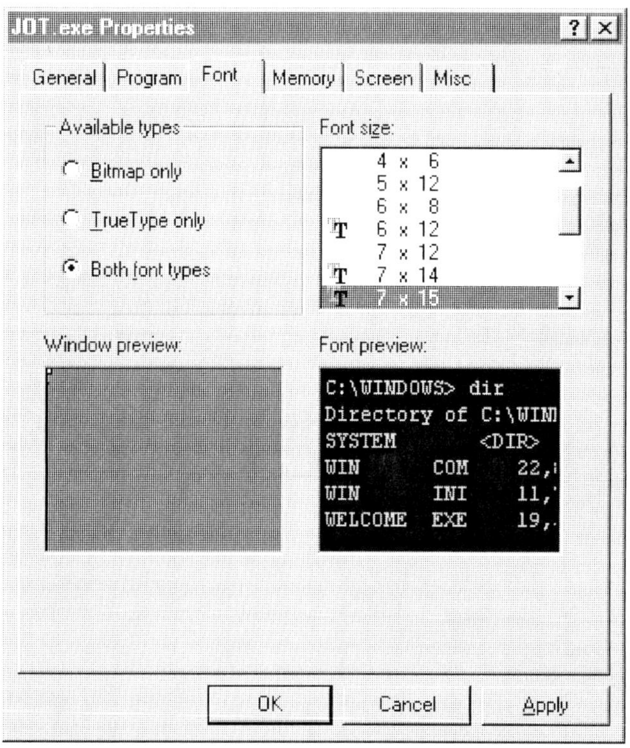

4. Memory properties

Memory management is a frequent problem for DOS applications. The options proposed in this window are those which were available in the versions 3.x of Windows. All types of memory are represented (EMS, XMS, DPMI) as is the space reserved for the environment variables (defined by using the MS-DOS command **SET variable=value**):

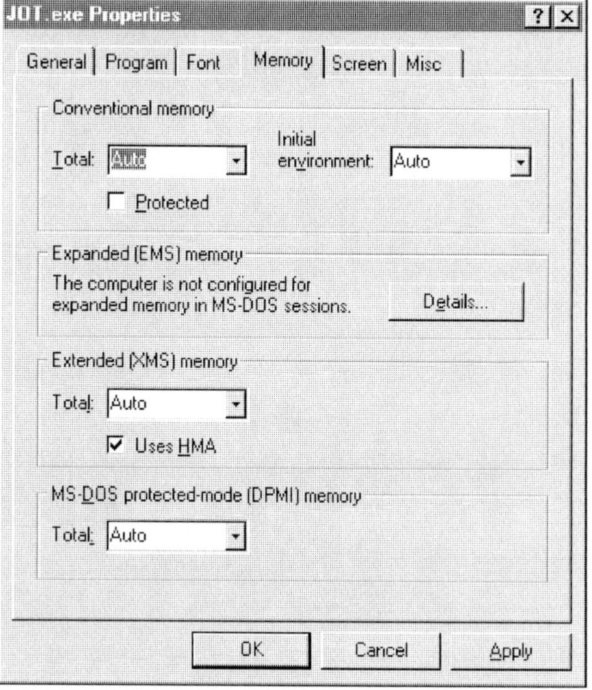

5. Screen properties

Some of the screen properties, such as whether or not the program should run in a window, were already available in the old PIF files. New options include the possibility of displaying the Windows tool bar in the application window:

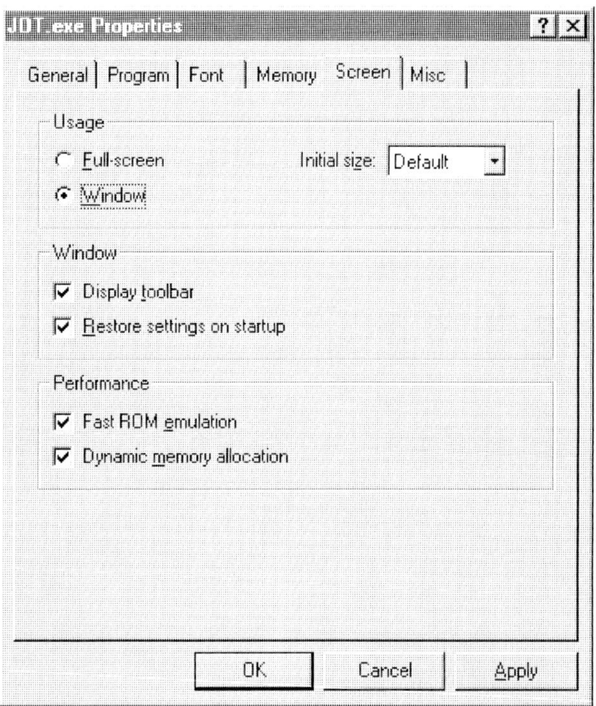

6. Miscellaneous properties

These allow you to define:

– whether or not the application display can be replaced by a screen saver if the application remains idle,
– the role of the mouse and whether of not it is exclusive to the application in question,
– the application's multitasking behaviour,
– the shortcut keys associated with the application.

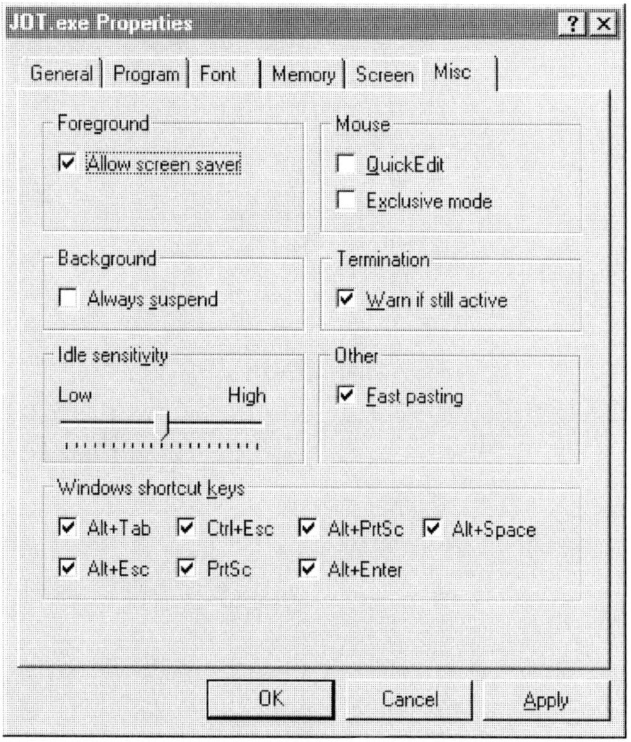

The network

Windows 95 networking has been devised to meet several criteria which have as much to do with the demands of the market place as they have with the necessity of anticipating the future.

Windows 95 networking functions are implemented with the following objectives in mind:

- to provide an internal architecture which is open, portable and able to evolve,
- to provide a universal network client service, which is compatible with all major systems on the market,
- to provide a simple means of configuration.

A. Network architecture under Windows 95 - WOSA

Currently, most manufacturers of networking components are working to achieve independence from the hardware by means of standardised system calls or some kind of additional layer which ensures compatibility. They are also realising that it is desirable to dissociate the system calls themselves from any particular transport protocol by adding one or more new layers. This would enable any application to use any network or service without having to employ several different APIs or, worse still, to manage different transports itself. This is the aim of WOSA (*Windows Open System Architecture*).

A standard application, a messaging system for instance, needs to provide the user with a unique, homogeneous way to send/receive messages, and to exploit the appropriate service providers.

Each service provider should be capable of sending the message over various networks and transports: local and remote networks, Ethernet networks, a FAX line...

The new layer introduced by WOSA is the *SPI (Service Provider Interface*). It complements the *API* (*Application Programming Interface*) used by the application.

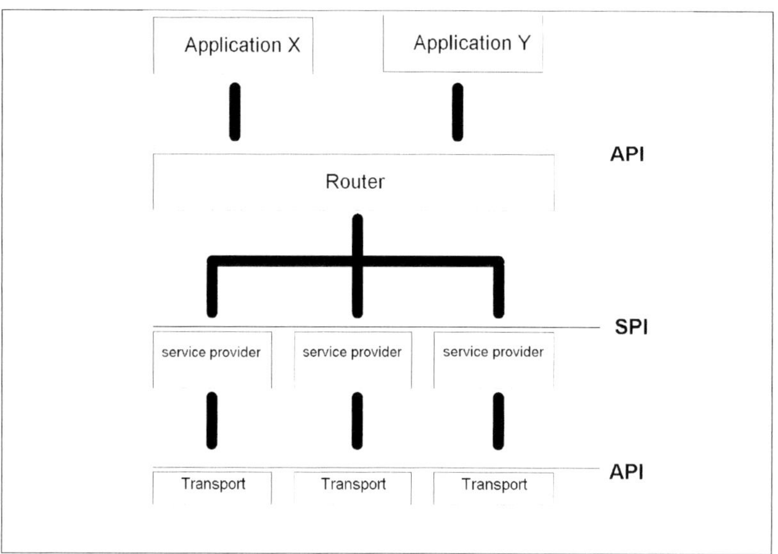

1. Layered architecture

A layered network structure, like the one defined on the OSI model, provides several advantages:

- dividing a problem into several parts makes it easier to solve.
- each module has fewer functions, but performs them perfectly.

It is barely thinkable today that one monolithic program could be created to deal with such a vast problem, which involves diverse elements such as network applications and the driver for the hardware adapter.

A layered architecture makes it much easier to optimise each layer. Ideally, hardware and software modules produced by different manufacturers and editors can interface with one another, as long as they respect the specifications of each layer. It is also possible to replace software located in one layer with other, more powerful software without the other layers being affected.

Windows 95 follows the dominant tendency and breaks down its networking features into seven layers:

Application interface	WIN32 WINNET		WIN32 printing API
Network support	Winnet 16	Netware support	Windows support
File system interface	Installable file system manager		
Redirectors/ services	Redirector	Services	
		Windows Sockets	
Transport programming NetBIOS interface	NetBios		
Transport protocols	TCP/IP	NetBEUI	IPX/SPX
Device driver interface	NDIS V 3.1		
	NDIS V2	ODI	

Application interface

This layer provides applications with a standard interface, WIN32, the successor to the WIN16 API. It is a subset of the WIN32 API available under Windows NT so allows developers to write applications which will run under both Windows 95 and Windows NT, provided that they do not exploit capacities specific to NT.

It provides services for access to remote resources, both disk and printer resources.

Network support layer

Even if Microsoft dominates the office software market, there are other editors and manufacturers of networking components who are too big to be ignored. A product like Windows 95 must cater for them.

Windows 95 is designed to be a universal client, supporting not only Microsoft networking (NT Server environment) but also Novell NetWare and UNIX.

The core version of Windows 95 includes networking features for:

- WINNET 16
  already in existence under Windows for Workgroups, it is only included for reasons of compatibility.
- NetWare
  Windows 95 can be either client or server for NetWare. Microsoft has entirely rewritten the NetWare client in 32 bits.
- Windows
  Windows 95 is a Windows client or server, providing disk sharing and printing services similar to those supplied by Workgroups. It can also be integrated into an NT Server domain where it is able to implement user-level security.

File system interface - IFS

All requests are channelled through the IFS manager. The advantage of this is that the underlying layers are concealed from the applications. One of the tasks assumed by the IFS manager is to engage the services of a local file system or, via the redirector, of a remote file system. All the higher functions, such as the memory cache, can be applied independently of the file system used.

Redirectors and services

This is the level at which an application request can be transformed into a call on the network's transport interface, if appropriate for the resource required. The Windows redirector uses Microsoft's *SMB* request format (*Server Message Block*), Whereas the NetWare redirector uses *NCP* packets (*NetWare Core Protocol*).

Various services are available at this level and yet more could be added in the future, if new products are developed by the software editors who are involved with the development of Windows 95. The services currently available are:

– file/printer sharing services (NetWare and Microsoft).
– remote printer driver service (*Remote Printer* from Hewlett Packard).
– network backup agent services (Cheyenne/Arcadia...).
– remote administration service - remote access to the registries....

Unlike NT Server, Windows 95 cannot be a Windows server and a NetWare server ***simultaneously****. Just one sharing service can run at a time.*

Transport programming interface

Early on, Microsoft showed a preference for the NetBIOS interface, which provides the means of writing network applications independently of the underlying communication protocol.

It is possible to perform NetBIOS calls with TCP/IP or IPX and, of course with NetBEUI, which is in fact a generalisation of the NetBIOS interface.

Sockets are supported too, but in the Microsoft context they are independent of the underlying protocol. This sets them apart from *Berkeley* Sockets, which remain closely associated with UNIX and TCP/IP.

The concepts involved, however, reflect the Berkeley specification. Microsoft has produced its version of the *stream*-type Socket, connected over TCP (*Transport Control Protocol*) and has kept the notion of the Socket datagram, based on *UDP* (*User Datagram Protocol*).

An example of a function call for the creation of a socket, in the Internet domain, based on the TCP protocol and so in reliable, connected mode:

```
s_tcp = socket( AF_INET, SOCK_STREAM,
IPPROTO_TCP );
```

If you are familiar with UNIX and Berkeley calls, you will notice a resemblance !

Transport protocols

Microsoft has never expressed a preference for a particular protocol, leaving the decision up to the network engineer. This tradition continues in Windows 95 and the three big transport protocols on the market are supplied with the core version:

- NetBEUI
- IPX/SPX
- TCP/IP

These three can coexist successfully under Windows 95.

NetBEUI is a very reliable and rapid protocol. It is non-routable, which restricts its use to local networks. It originates from research carried out for IBM by Sytek in the 80s. It is extremely simple to implement and suits *peer to peer* networks perfectly.

NetBEUI architecture

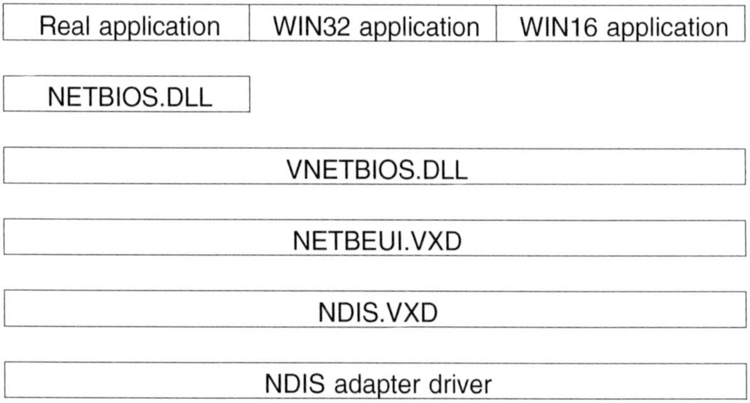

Real application	WIN32 application	WIN16 application

NETBIOS.DLL

VNETBIOS.DLL

NETBEUI.VXD

NDIS.VXD

NDIS adapter driver

IPX/SPX are, traditionally, the protocols used in NetWare environments. They are routable and rapid, but otherwise they only bring tangible advantages to systems which connect to this type of network (Novell 2, 3 and 4.x).

SPX provides reliable transport in connected mode, whereas IPX is datagram orientated. From a functional point of view, they can be compared to TCP and UDP repectively.

IPX/SPX architecture

WIN32 sockets application	IPX/SPX application	NetBIOS application in real mode ? NETBIOS.DLL VNETBIOS.DLL NXNBLINK.VXD	NetBIOS WIN16 or WIN32 application
WSOCK32. DLL		NETBIOS.DLL	
WSOCK. VXD		VNETBIOS.DLL	
WSIPX.VXD		NWNBLINK.VXD	
NWLINK.VXD			
NDIS.VXD			
NDIS 3.1 adapter driver			

Currently, the universal protocol de facto is TCP/IP, since it is the world's most widely used protocol and, in particular, it is the protocol of the world-wide network, the INTERNET. Strictly speaking, it is not a protocol but a complex and powerful suite of utilities and protocols. It takes its name from its two main norms, TCP and IP. These were developed originally for UNIX environments:

TCP	Transport Control Protocol
IP	Internet Protocol
UDP	User Datagram Protocol
ARP	Address Resolution Protocol
RARP	Reverse Address Resolution Protocol
FTP	File Transfer Protocol
TELNET	Terminal EmuLation over the NETwork
ICMP	Internet Control Message Protocol
SNMP	Simple Network Management Protocol
SMTP	Simple Mail Transfer Protocol

TCP/IP architecture

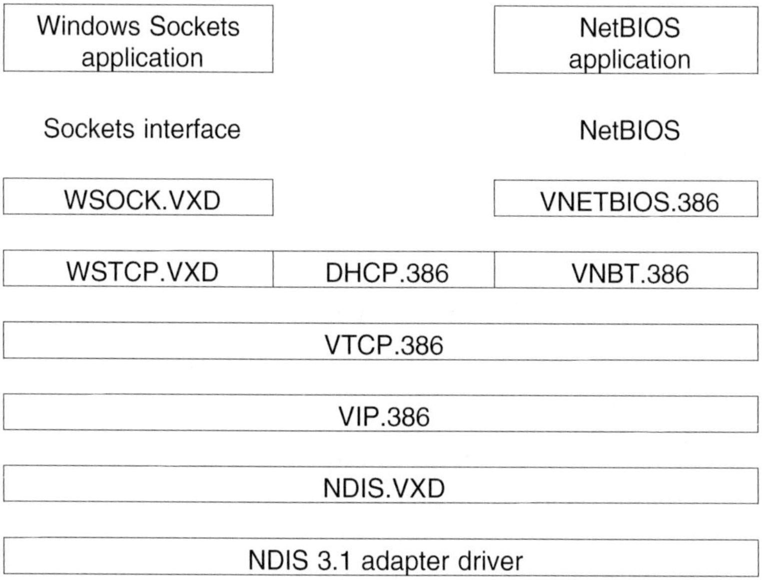

Windows Sockets application		NetBIOS application
Sockets interface		NetBIOS
WSOCK.VXD		VNETBIOS.386
WSTCP.VXD	DHCP.386	VNBT.386
VTCP.386		
VIP.386		
NDIS.VXD		
NDIS 3.1 adapter driver		

The distinguishing feature of TCP/IP implementation in Microsoft networks, and in particular with Windows 95, is the possibility of using DHCP (*Dynamic Host Configuration Protocol*).

A common criticism of TCP/IP is that IP addressing is relatively complicated. Each workstation must have a unique address, which includes addresses both for the network and for the workstation.

On condition that there is an NT Server in the network, the DHCP protocol makes it possible to allocate, dynamically, addresses to computers that request them. The addresses are taken from a scope reserved on the server. They are *leased* for a duration set by the administrator. This eliminates all potential address conflicts and makes TCP/IP as simple to implement as NetBEUI or IPX. UNIX's DNS (*Domain Name Server*) is also supported and the WINS service can be used for mapping NetBIOS names onto IP addresses.

In performance terms, notice the quality of the Microsoft implementation, which for a 13 Mb transfer of files over the network, gives a difference of just 7% between NetBEUI transport and TCP/IP !

Device driver interface

Still in favour with Microsoft, NDIS (Network Device Interface Specification) now exists in version 3.1 under Windows 95, which brings to it the functions of a Plug and Play driver. Notice too that a driver can control several cards even though it has only been loaded once into the memory (virtualisation).

The NDIS 3 specification already constituted an important advance as far as memory is concerned, since it supplied the means of driving an adapter in protected mode (VXD) whereas NDIS 2 constituted a real-mode driver interface.

B. Network configuration

Immensely simplified, the network configuration can be defined in either of two ways:

☞ 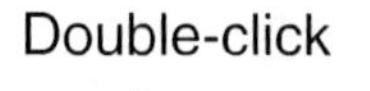 Double-click My Computer, then 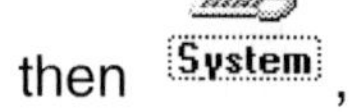 System,  Control Panel and lastly 

.

Or

Right-click the 

icon, then click **Properties**.

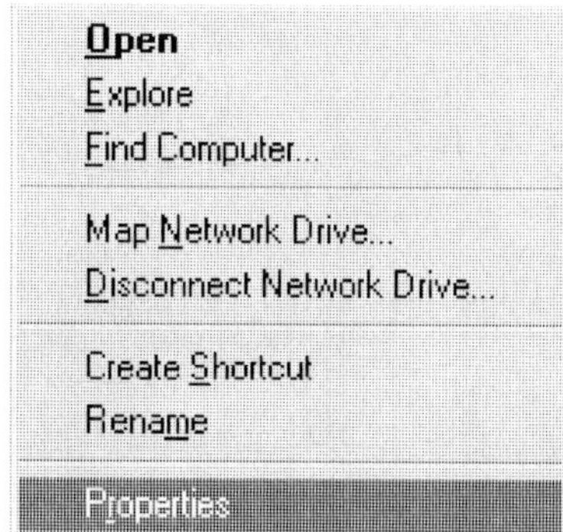

↓personal notes↓

In the next dialog box you can add or remove network software or hardware, or change its properties:

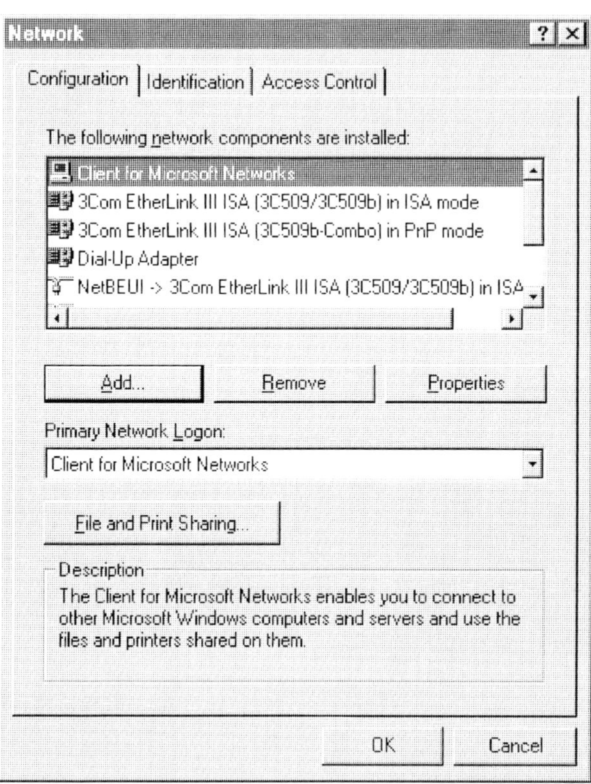

☞ Click the **Add** button to add a component :

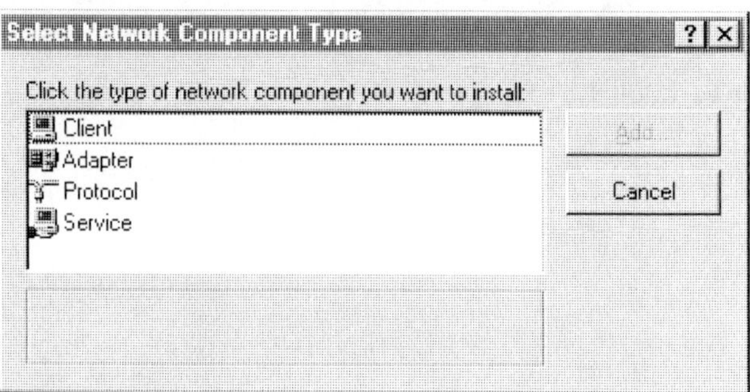

There are four components which can be added:
- Client
- Adapter
- Protocol
- Service

1. Adding clients

You can add clients supplied by Microsoft, or clients from other editors:

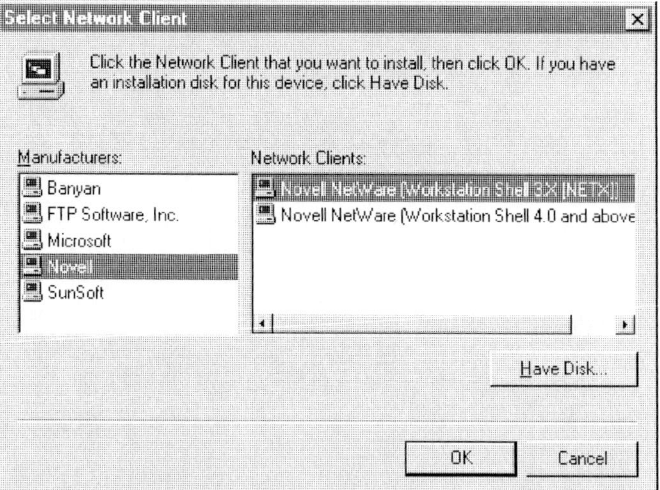

For clients other than those supplied by Microsoft (the Novell client and the Microsoft client), you need the appropriate client software, for example, PC-NFS from SunSoft.

After installing the client software, click the **Properties** button to define its configuration.

2. Adding an adapter

The same dialog box provides a simple way of adding an adapter :

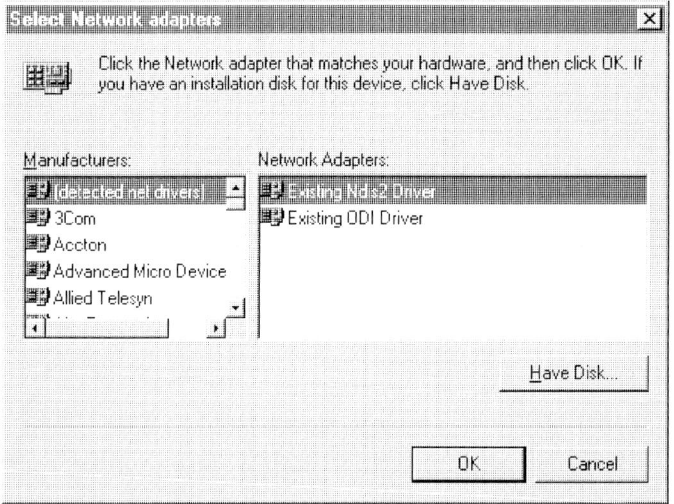

Configuring the adapter

The properties of the adapter are divided into four groups under four different tabs:

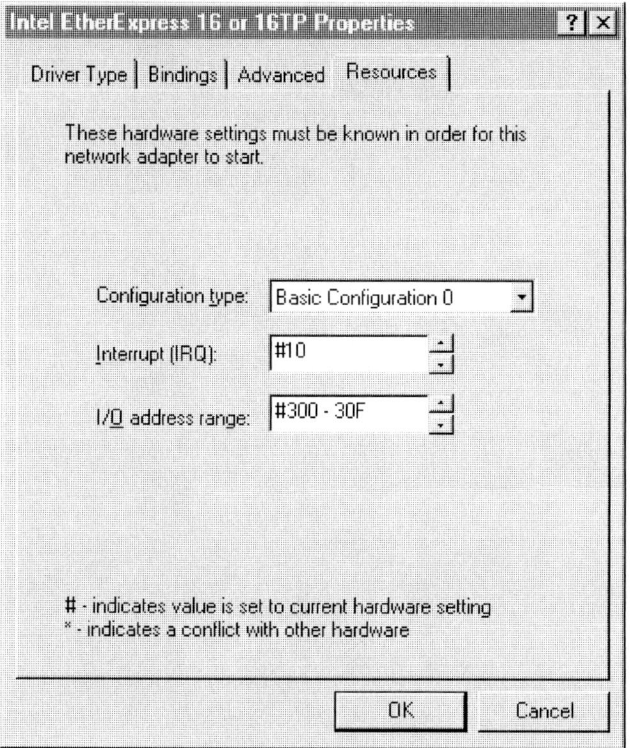

Driver Type

On the **Driver Type** page, choose to install either NDIS drivers (in 32-bit protected mode or in 16-bit real mode) or ODI drivers (NetWare).

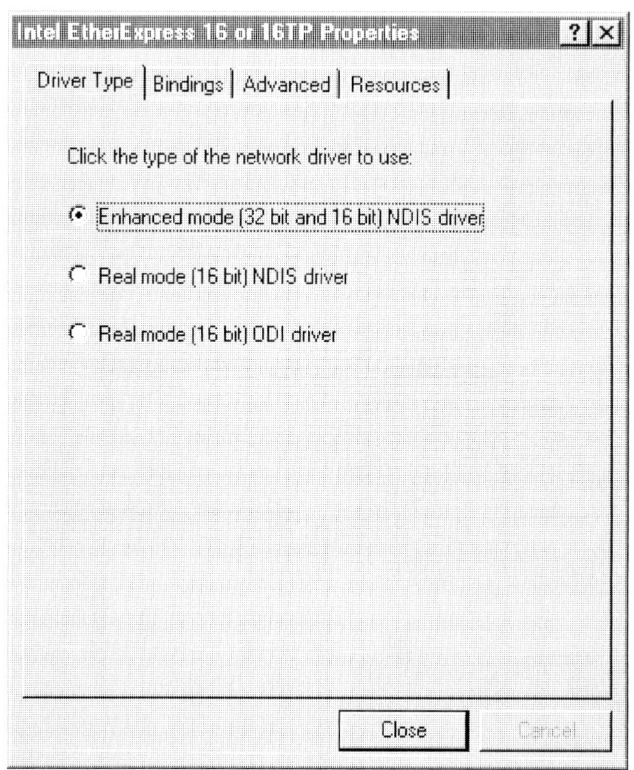

Bindings

Under the **Bindings** tab, there are options for deactivating individual protocols on individual adapters. It is possible to limit the use of a particular protocol to a particular section of the network:

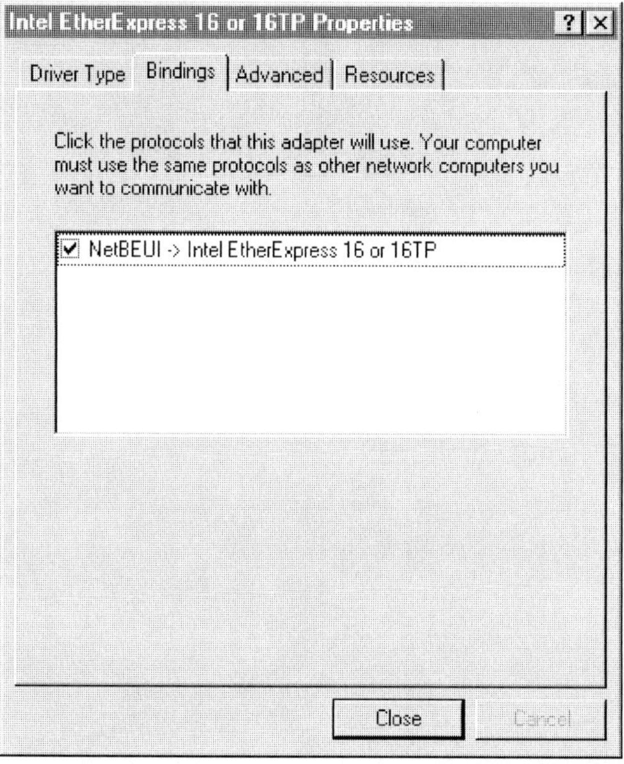

↓personal notes↓

Advanced

The **Advanced** properties' role is to deal with various particularities of specific adapters; *transceiver* type, twisted pair...

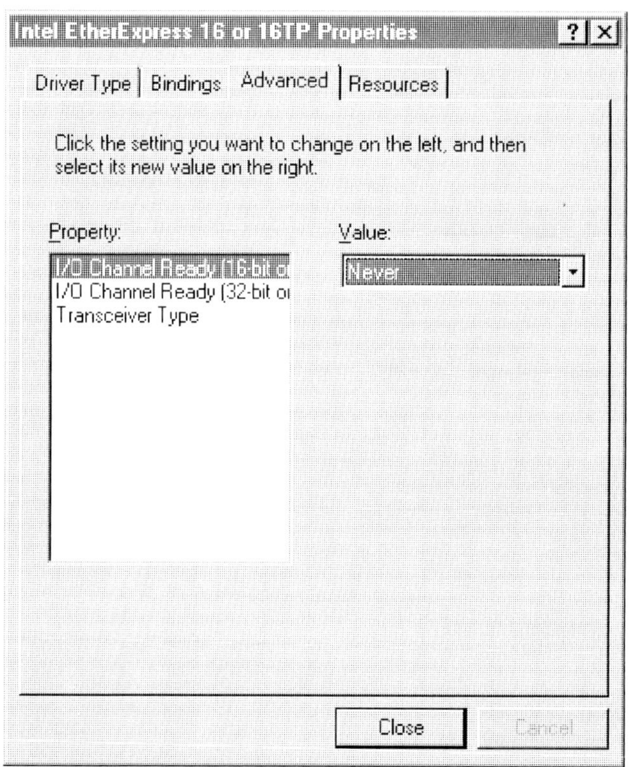

Resources

The **Resource** page groups together options for defining the interrupt used by the adapter and I/O addresses:

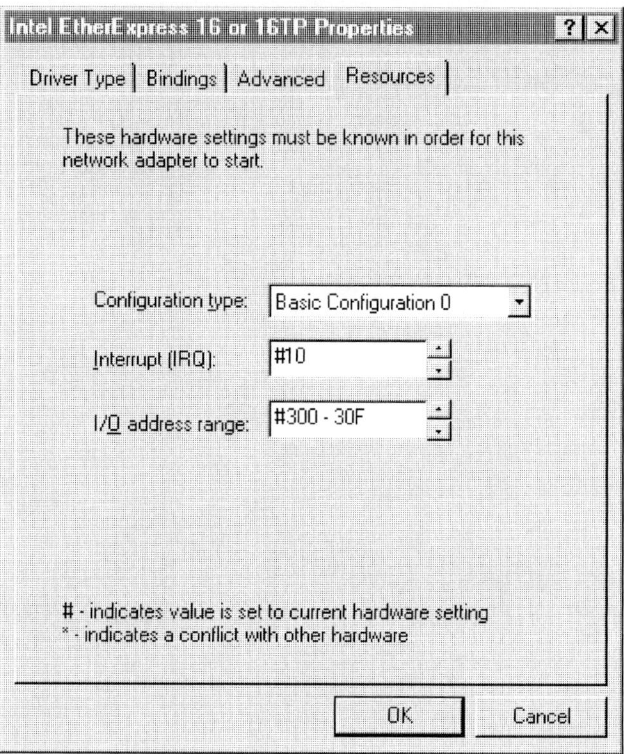

3. Adding a protocol

There is also an **Add** button which allows you to add a protocol. Once again, it is possible to add protocols marketed by various editors, in addition to those supplied by Microsoft:

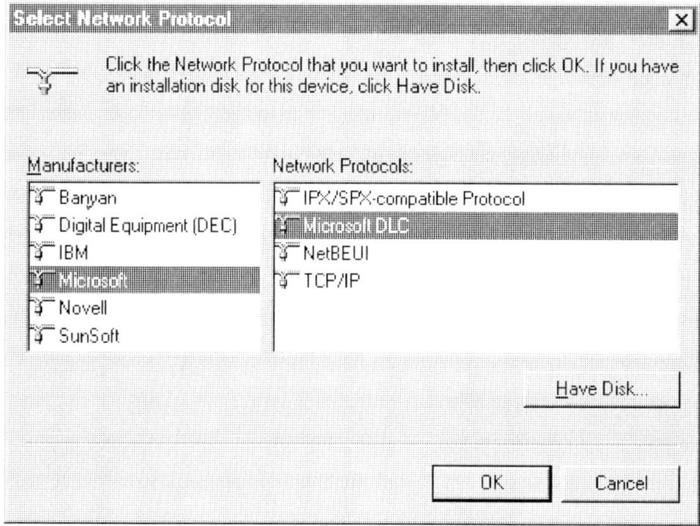

It is worth mentioning that the **DLC** (*Data Link Control*) protocol is available in this window. It is used for communicating with network printers (LaserJet Si among others) and with some IBM equipment.

Configuring the protocol

Once you have added the protocol you require, you can display its properties. With TCP/IP, for instance, this property sheet is where you determine whether to set a static address yourself, or to obtain an address dynamically from DHCP:

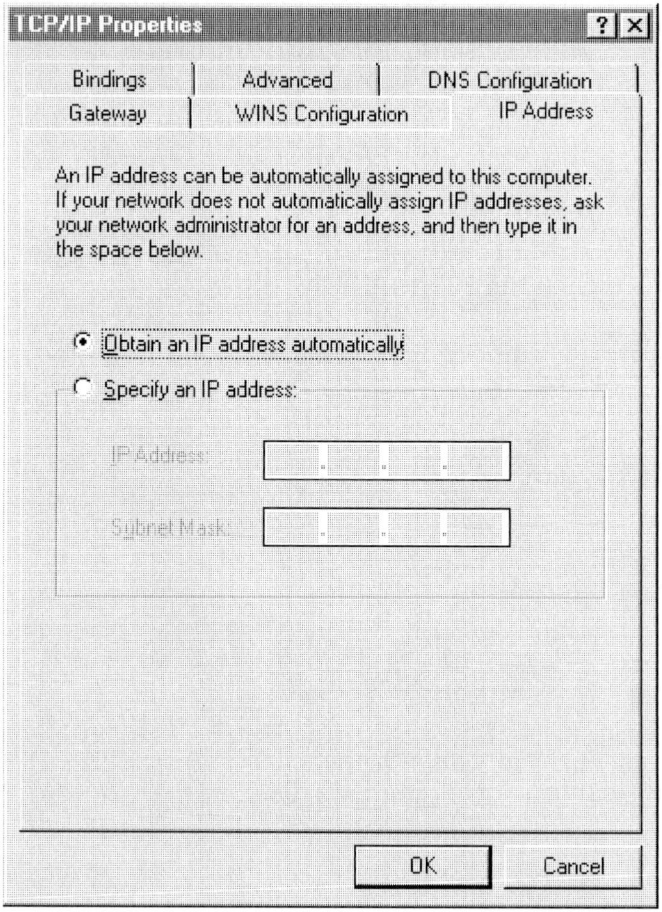

TCP/IP Properties

Bindings | Advanced | DNS Configuration

Gateway | WINS Configuration | IP Address

An IP address can be automatically assigned to this computer. If your network does not automatically assign IP addresses, ask your network administrator for an address, and then type it in the space below.

Obtain an IP address automatically

Specify an IP address:

IP Address:

Subnet Mask:

OK Cancel

If you have access to an NT Server machine acting as a **DHCP** server, this option eliminates the risk of a conflict of IP addresses.

4. Adding services

The last in the list of network modules that can be added, services too can be Microsoft products, or acquired from other editors.

Among those supplied by Microsoft, there are disk and printer sharing services for both Microsoft and NetWare Networks.

As mentioned earlier, Microsoft and NetWare file/printer-sharing services cannot coexist on the same machine, as they can under NT Server:

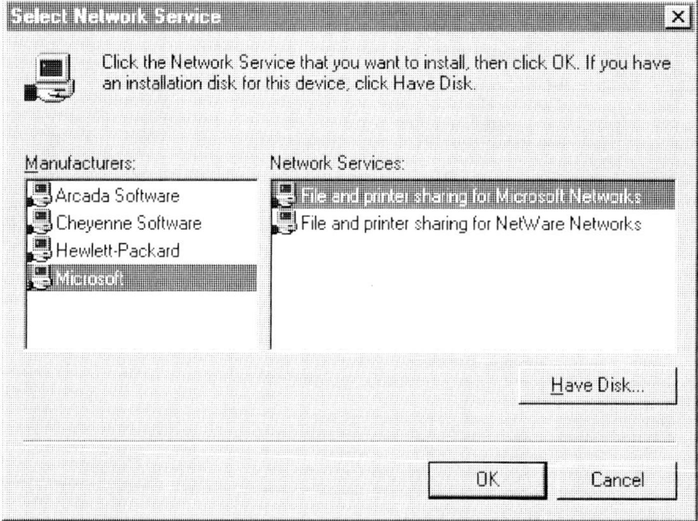

You can use the **File and Print Sharing** button to deactivate a disk or printer sharing service for a Windows 95 workstation.

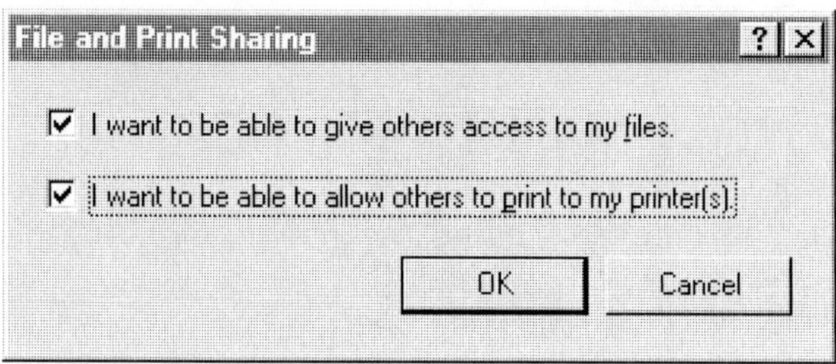

The properties for file and printer sharing can be edited to define:

– the LM announce
  does the workstation declare itself as a server for LAN Manager clients ?
– the role of the workstation
  (Browse Master or not) this option can be set to **Enabled**, **Disabled** or **Automatic**.

Indicate whether of not you want the workstation to act as browse master, or select **Automatic** for the browse master to be chosen in an election.

If you choose **Automatic**, an NT machine will always take precedence over a 95 machine, which itself takes precedence over a Workgroups machine. If an NT Server machine is available, especially if it is a domain controller, it will always be elected browse master for the domain.

There always has to be one machine which acts as browse master in a workgroup or a domain. On an individual computer, setting the browse master option to **Disabled** can improve speed up operations, since keeping the list of resources for browsing is a time-consuming operation.

Browsing is used when, for example, a user requests a connection to a network drive, or wants to look through the resources on a drive which is connected. The workstation obtains, from the browse master, the list of machines in the workgroup or domain.

C. Monitoring network activity

1. The net watcher

The net watcher shows you all the different shares on a workstation and any uses who are connected to them. This makes it possible to find out which files are currently open and which user is working with them. This information can be supplied for the local machine or for a remote machine configured for remote administration.

The default installation does not install the net watcher. It can be installed once the system is running by starting the **Add/Remove Programs** procedure.

After installation, it can be reached via the **Start** menu:

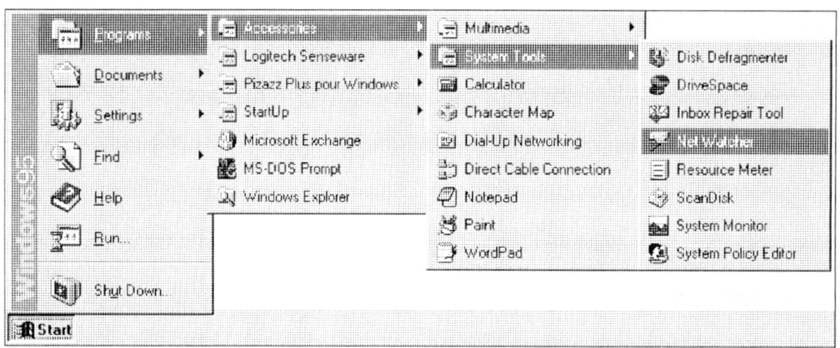

Displaying the users who are connected

To see the list of users who are currently connected :

☞ **View**
by Connections

You might need to refresh the data displayed by pressing the F5 key or by **View - Refresh**:

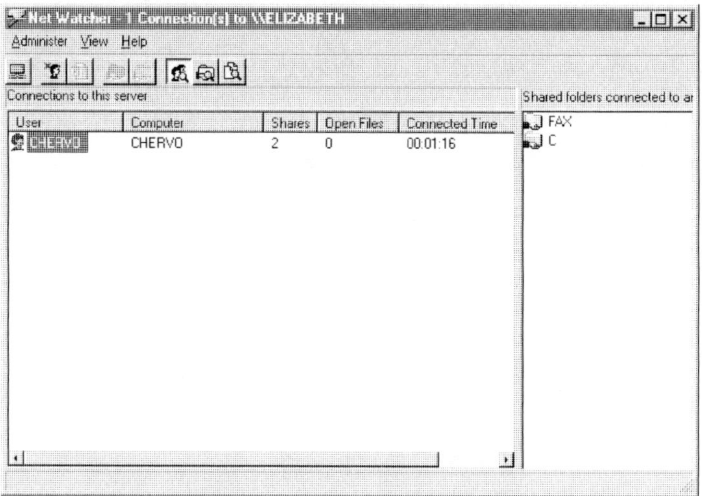

Displaying shared resources

☞ **View**
by Shared Folders

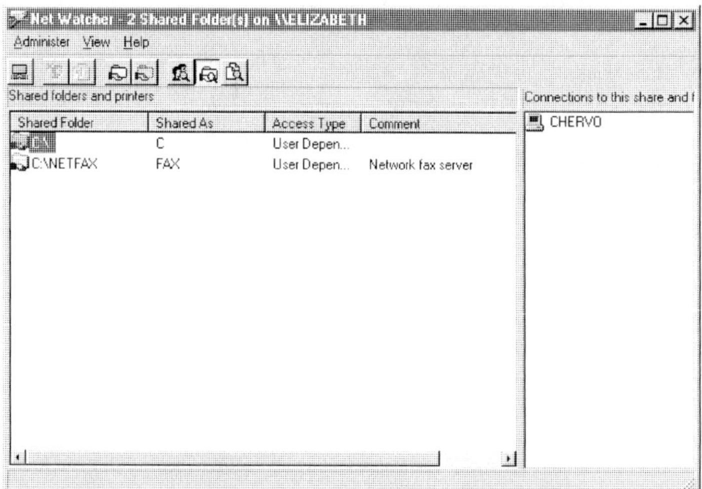

Displaying files opened by other users

☞ **View**
by Open Files

Details of all open files are displayed, along with the mode in which they have been opened:

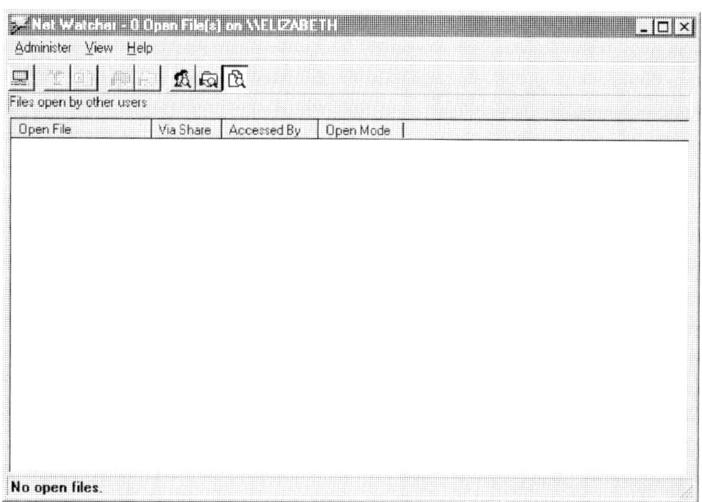

Implementing remote administration

Authorising remote administration

Before a workstation can be administered over the network, you must go through the following steps:

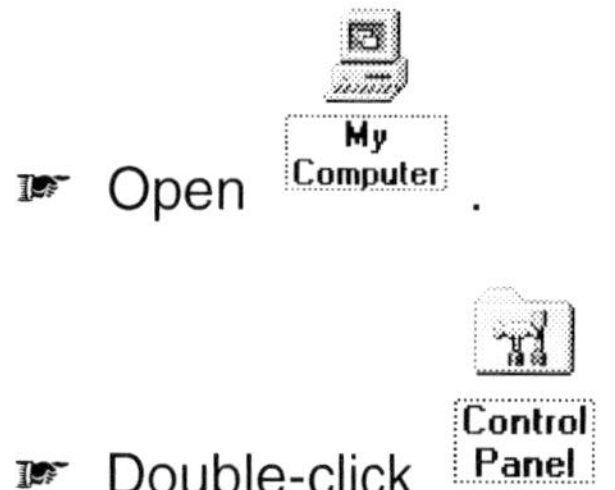

☞ Open My Computer.

☞ Double-click Control Panel.

☞ Choose Passwords .

☞ Click the **Remote Administration** tab and activate the **Enable Remote Administration of this server** check box.

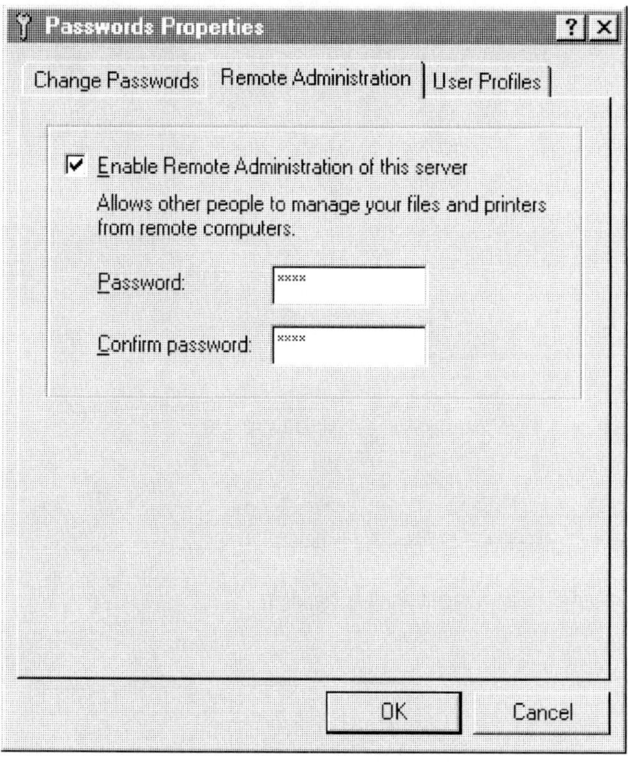

Putting remote administration into action

From another computer, you can now use the net watcher to see how the machine, where you have activated remote administration, is being used and even to modify the shares defined on it:

☞ **Administer**
Select Server

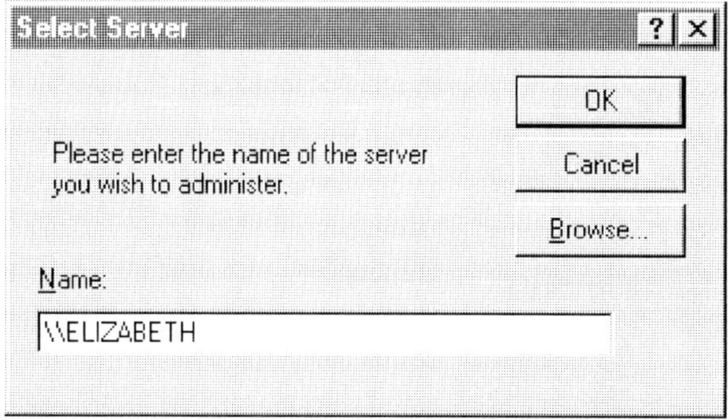

☞ Give the name of the server in UNC (*Universal Naming Convention*) format, then enter.

Creating a share on a remote machine

To create a new share on a remote machine where remote administration is implemented:

☞ **View**
by Shared Folders

☞ **Administer**
Add Shared Folder

☞ Enter the physical path to the new share, or use the **Browse** button.

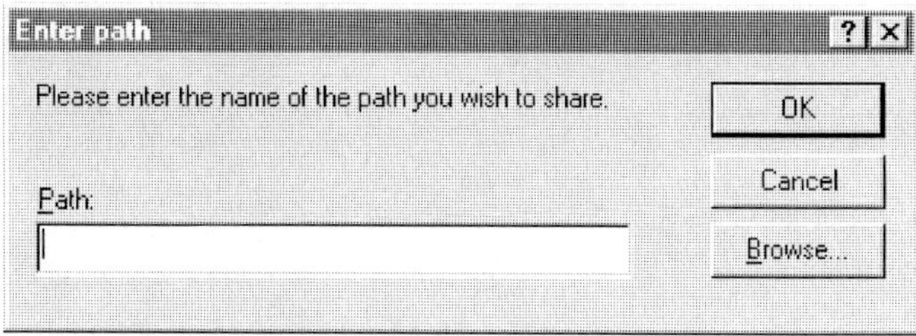

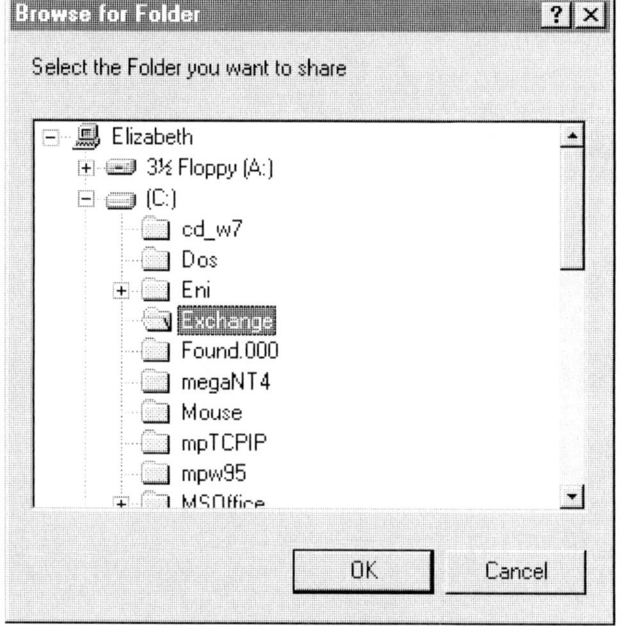

☞ Click **OK** to validate the new share.

☞ Activate the **Shared As** option button then give the name of the new share, and the type of access authorised:

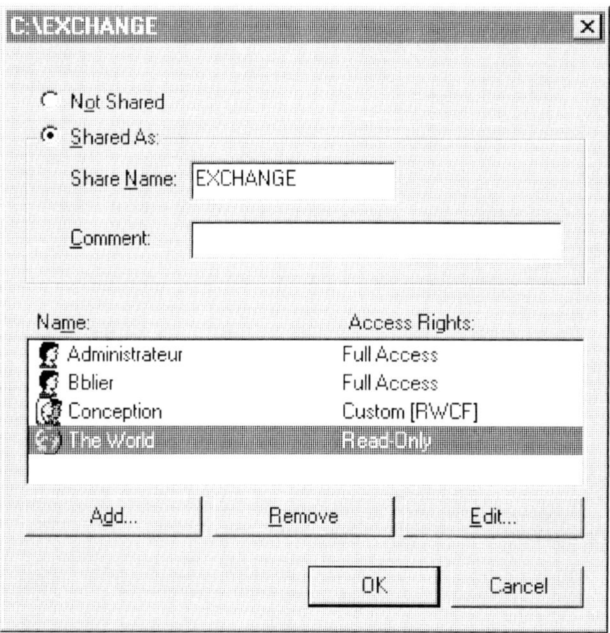

Ceasing to share a remote resource

To put an end to the remote share of a folder:

☞ Select the resource from the list of shares.

☞ **Administer**
Stop Sharing Folder

☞ Click the **Yes** button to validate the operation.

Editing the properties of a share

In the property sheet, you can change the type of access or the passwords for a folder.

☞ Select the share in question.

☞ **Administer**
Shared Folder Properties [Alt][Entrée]

D. Integration into an NT Server domain

Although workstations under Windows 95 function perfectly in a peer to peer network, or *workgroup*, it is nonetheless true that Windows 95 is the ideal client for a domain controlled by an NT Server computer. As a client of NT Server, the 95 workstation benefits from additional security features (among others). As soon as the number of users exceeds five to ten, you should think about abandoning the peer to peer structure and adopting a domain-type organisation.

1. The domain: a definition

A domain is a group of machines which includes:

- one (no more, no less) NT Server computer which acts as *Primary Domain Controller*. On this machine, the original of the user accounts database is located. The accounts database enables users to obtain permissions on any machine in the domain: each user is identified once only, by a name and a password.
- As an option (but a highly recommended one...), one or more *Backup Domain Controllers* each of which has a copy of the user accounts database and participates in validating accesses.
- Any number of client workstations.

2. Integrating a Windows 95 workstation into a domain

To log on to a Windows NT Server domain, you should go through the following procedure:

☞ Double-click My Computer then open Control Panel.

☞ Double-click the Network icon.

☞ Select the **Client for Microsoft networks** component (or add it if it is not already installed) and display its properties.

☞ Activate the **Log on to Windows NT domain** check box and give the name of the domain:

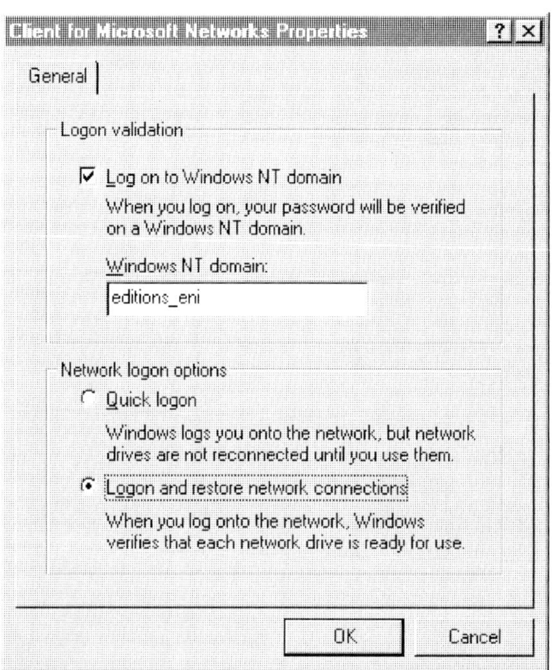

☞ Click **OK** to confirm.

If you want to, modify the option for your primary network logon. The option you choose determines whether the domain's account database is necessarily used to validate your user name and password:

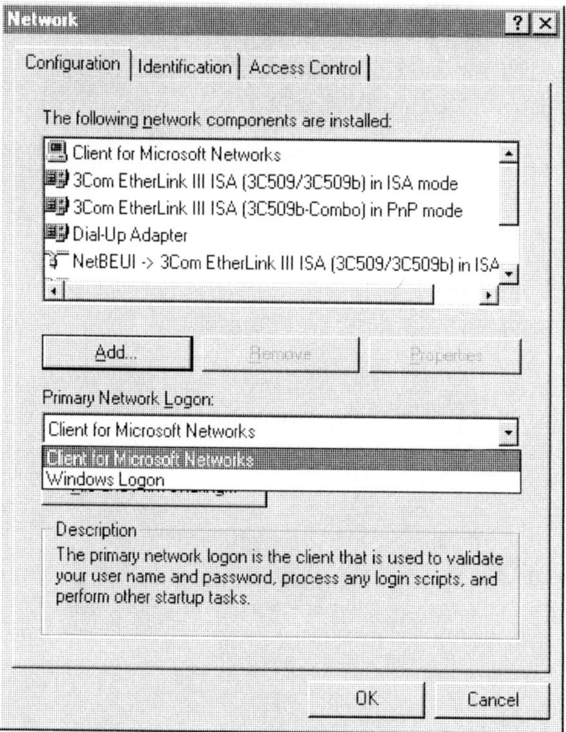

E. Security

Traditionally, Microsoft networks provide two types of security, which already existed in LAN Manager:
- share-level security
- user-level security

Share-level security involves setting access permissions for a shared resource by means of a password. Anyone who learns the password can access the resource. It is not possible to determine precisely who can or cannot use the resource.
Windows for Workgroups, for example, applies only this type of security.

User-level security makes it possible to assign specific permissions to an individual user, identified by a unique user name/password combination. This type of security is closer to traditional systems in its approach.

NT Server uses this type of security, which allows much greater precision in assigning permissions and more effective control.

Windows 95 is able to implement both types of security, but not in every case. In fact, user-level security can only be applied if the Windows 95 workstation is integrated into an NT Server domain, where it can refer to the accounts database.

By default, Windows 95 applies share-level security.

To apply user-level security:

☞ Go into My Computer then open Control Panel.

☞ Double-click .

☞ Click the **Access Control** tab then activate **User-level access control**:

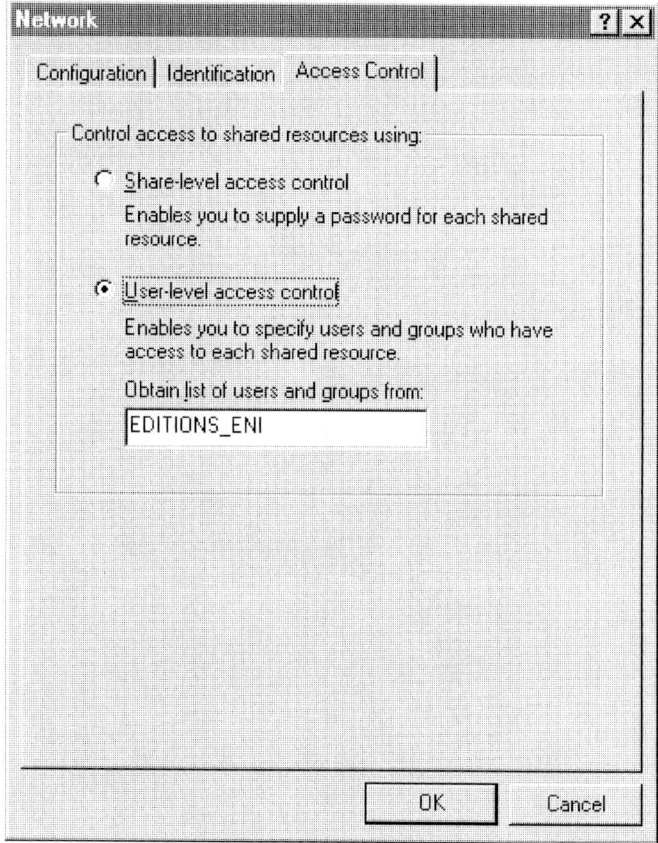

☞ Indicate the domain from which the user accounts can be obtained and click **OK**.

At this point, you can create a new share and indicate who is authorised to access it:

- Go into 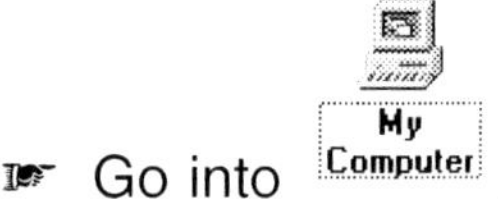

.
- Double-click the icon which represents the disk 

.
- Right-click the folder you want to share, and take the **Sharing** option from the shortcut menu.

In the dialog box which appears, you can share the folder and, by clicking the **Add** button, you can choose the users who can access it, and set their level of permissions:

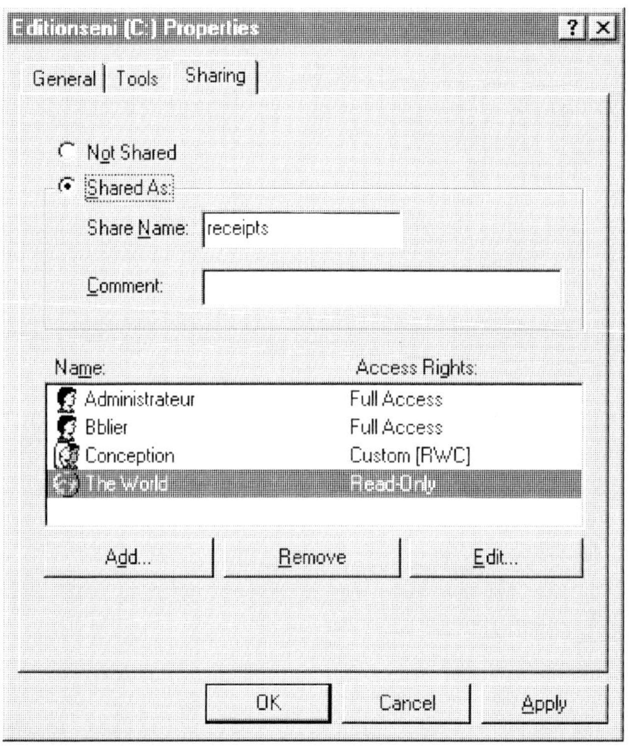

1. User Profiles

Like windows NT, Windows 95 has the advantage of managing user profiles.

A user profile can contain the following elements:

- desktop settings (colours, background...)
- shortcut icons (but not their arrangement on the desktop...).
- contents of the **Start** menu.
- program groups and preferences.

Several users work at the same machine. Each user can has his/her own environment. The user identifies himself at logon and his environment is produced.

- In this case the profiles are **local profiles**.
- A single user works with several machines in an NT domain. He/she can have the same environment whatever the machine. Profiles of this type are called **roaming profiles**.

This is almost a return to the intelligent terminal !

Setting up local profiles

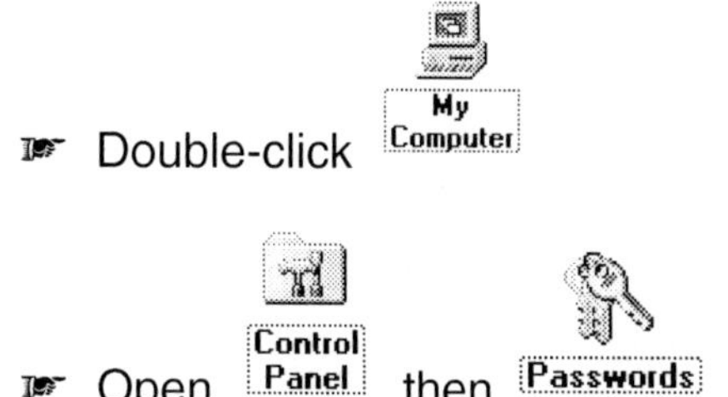

☞ Double-click My Computer

☞ Open Control Panel then Passwords

☞ Click the **User Profiles** tab and select the second option button to activate user profiles. If you want to include extra items in the profile, click the appropriate check box:

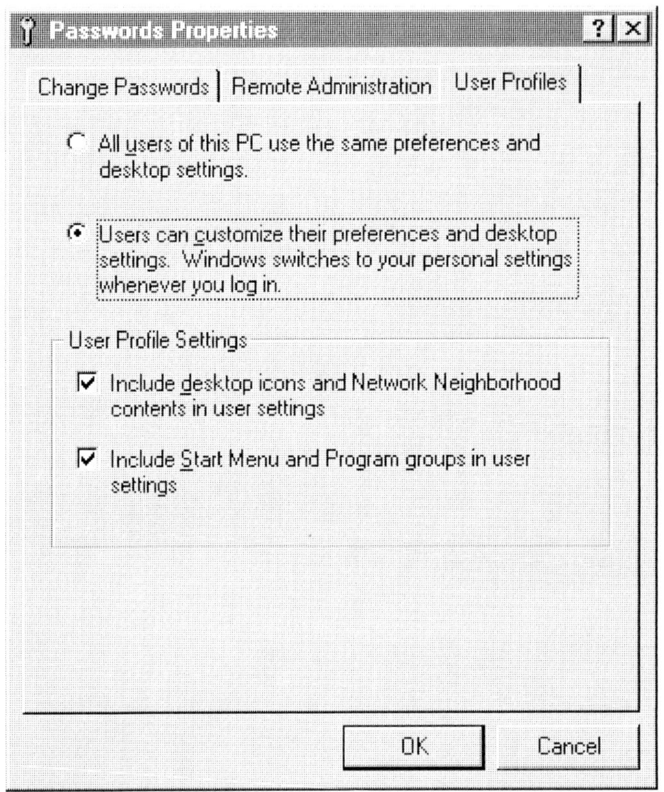

☞ Click **OK**.

The next time a user logs on to the machine, he or she will need to give a user name and password:

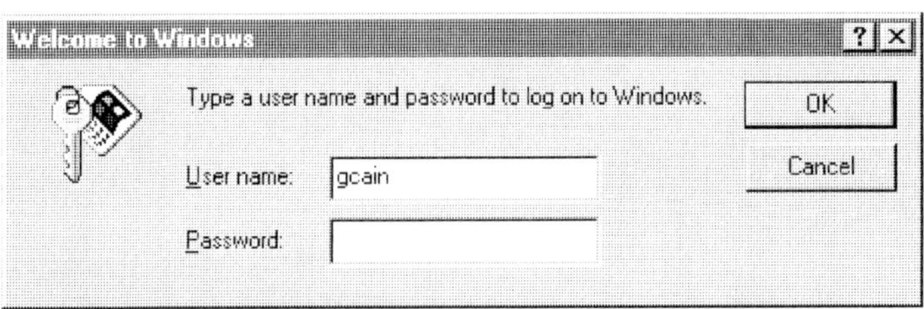

The next window which appears concerns user profiles:

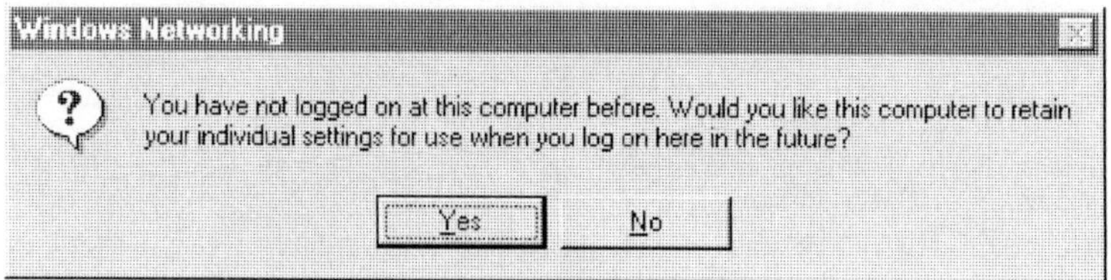

☞ Click **OK** to enter.

The various users of the computer can each retrieve their own environment.

Setting up roaming profiles on the server

Operations to perform on the Windows 95 workstations

First of all, activate local profiles on the Windows 95 workstations.
Check that each user logs onto an NT Server domain as a client for Microsoft networks and that this logon is the principle network logon:

☞ Right-click the 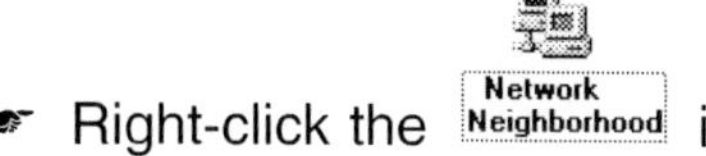 icon.

↓personal notes↓

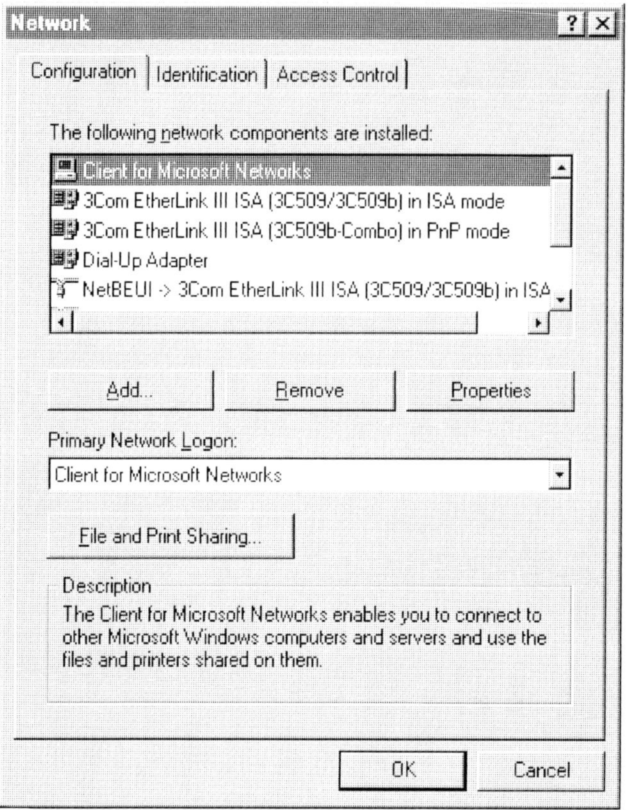

☞ Click **Client for Microsoft Networks** then the **Properties** button.

- Activate the logon check box and give the name of the domain.

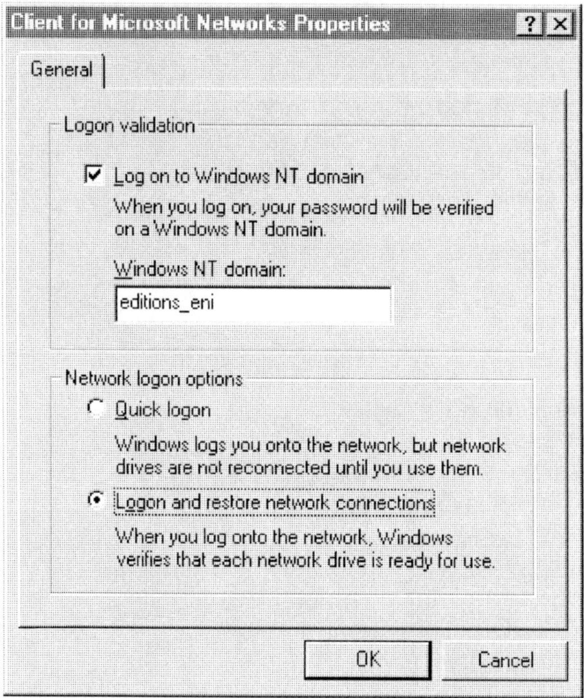

- Click **OK**.

Operations to perform on one of the domain controllers

- Start the **User Manager for Domains** by means of the  icon.

- In the list which appears, double-click the name of the user for whom you are creating the profile.

- Click the **Profile** button then give the home directory: this is a network drive corresponding to a valid UNC path, usually \\SERVER\USERS\%USERNAME%.
- Click **OK** to confirm then leave the User Manager for Domains.

The user in question can log onto the domain from any of its Windows 95 machines, and work in his/her own environment. This environment is stored in the user's working directory on the server, as a hierarchy including the **Start** menu, desktop parameters, colours...

2. System policies

The purpose of system policies is to limit the actions which a user can perform in the control panel and in the desktop settings. They also make it possible to customise part of the user's environment. You can even exploit them to restrict a user to specific applications.

The system policies are stored either in a machine's *registry* or in a file named CONFIG.POL. This second solution has the advantage of greater flexibility.

Policy information is only stored in the registry if there is no network server, or if the computer concerned is a stand alone machine.

Location of the policies file

The CONFIG.POL file can be stored at various locations:

By default, Windows 95 looks in the directory where it is installed (C:\WINDOWS) for this file.

If the network server is an NT Server machine, the CONFIG.POL file must be situated in the NETLOGON share of the server which corresponds to the path (%SYSTEMROOT%\SYSTEM32\REPL\IMPORT\
SCRIPTS), so that it can be downloaded automatically at logon.

If you are using a NetWare server, you should put the file in the PUBLIC directory of the SYS volume.

When a CONFIG.POL file exists, it systematically takes precedence over any policy data in the registry. A policy saved in the registry is overridden by a policy in a .POL file.

Computer policy, group policy, user policy

A policy can be defined for:
- an individual user,
- a group of users (if you are working in a network),
- a machine.

Default user, default computer

There are a user and computer which apply if no new user, group or computer has been defined. New users take on the basic characteristics set for the default user, and specific elements can be defined precisely for this user.

Installing files for managing system policy

The files and tools for managing system policy are located on the Windows 95 CD ROM, in the directory \ADMIN\APTOOLS\POLEDIT.

Client machines

On client machines, the machines which will be subject to system policy restrictions, you must not install the utility for creating and editing policies, POLEDIT.EXE, but only the client side elements:

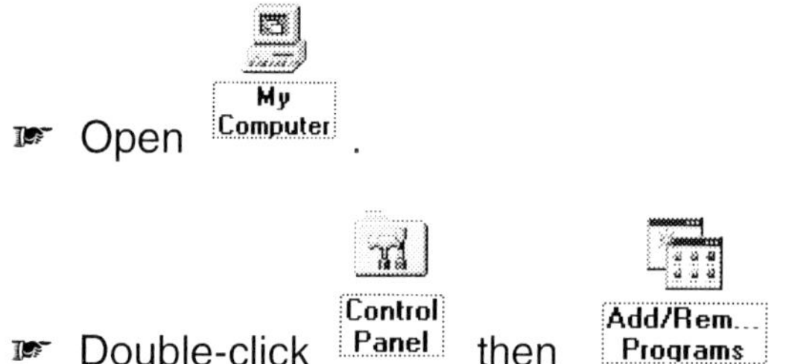

- Open .
- Double-click then .
- Click the Windows setup tab then click the **Have Disk** button.
- Give the path to the directory on the CD-ROM which contains POLEDIT:

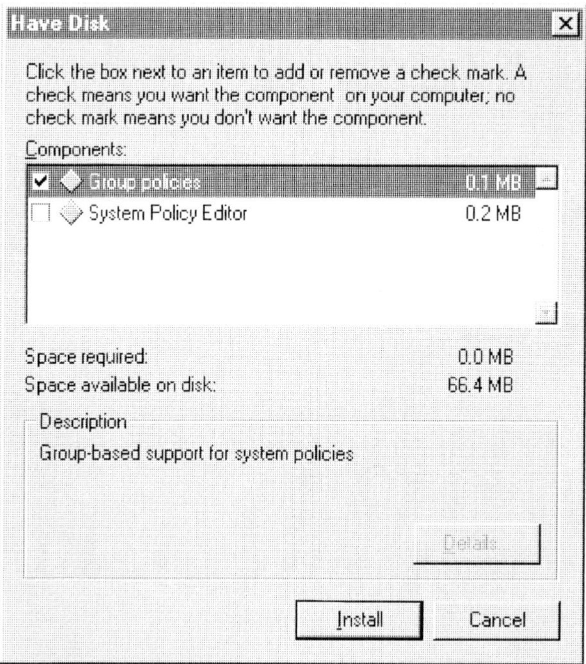

The administrator machine

On the administrator machine, you need to install the group policies and also POLEDIT, the system policy editor:

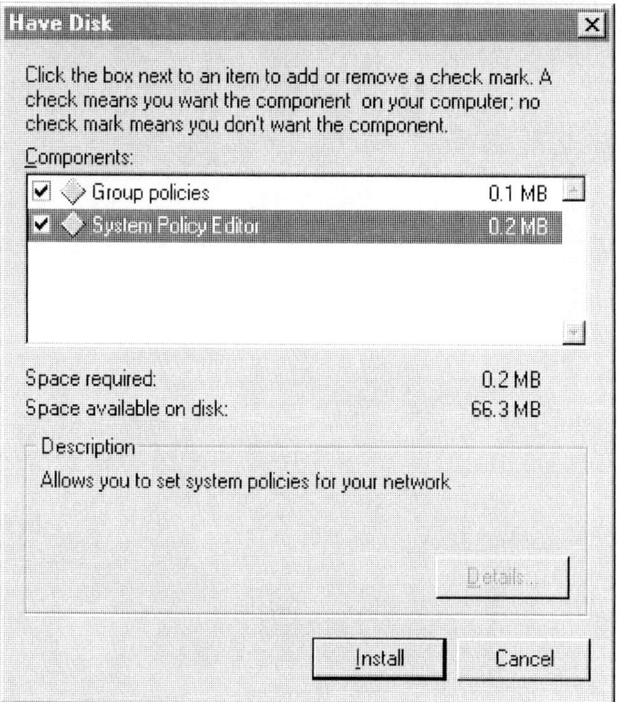

↓personal notes↓

Creating a policies file: CONFIG.POL

☞ Start POLEDIT.EXE by clicking.

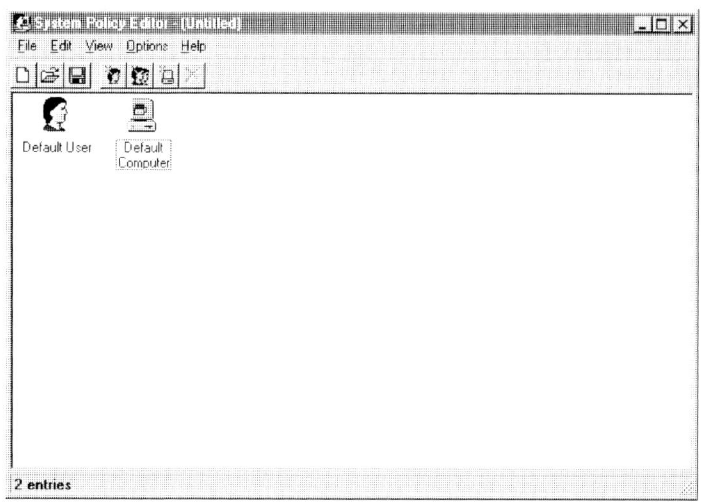

Creating a user or a group

☞ **Edit**
Add User/Group

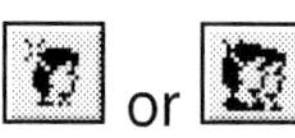

☞ Enter the name of the user/group or use the **Browse** button to look through the names of users and groups in the domain:

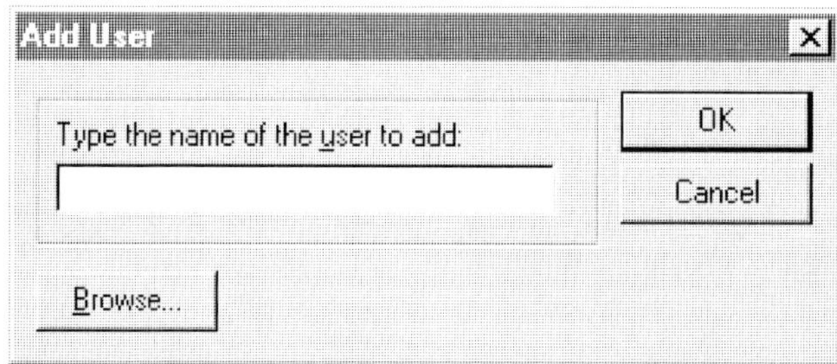

☞ Click the **Add** button then **OK** to add the selected user or group.

Creating a computer

This stage is only necessary if you need to apply extraordinary security to a particular computer, for example, one which is accessible to the public.

To create the computer:

☞ **Edit**
Add Computer

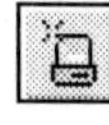

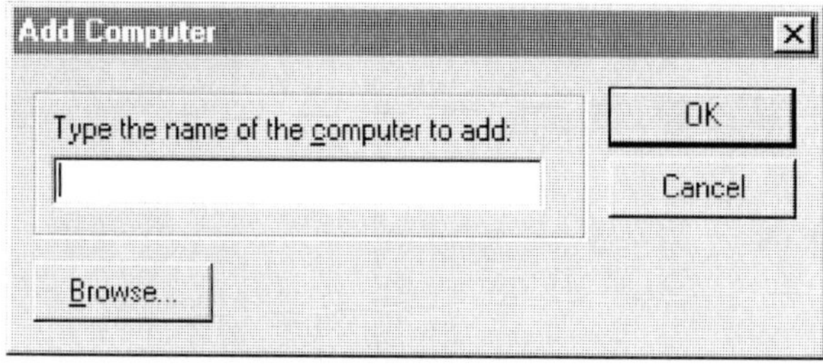

☞ Enter the name of the machine or use the **Browse** button to select the machine from the list of those in the network:

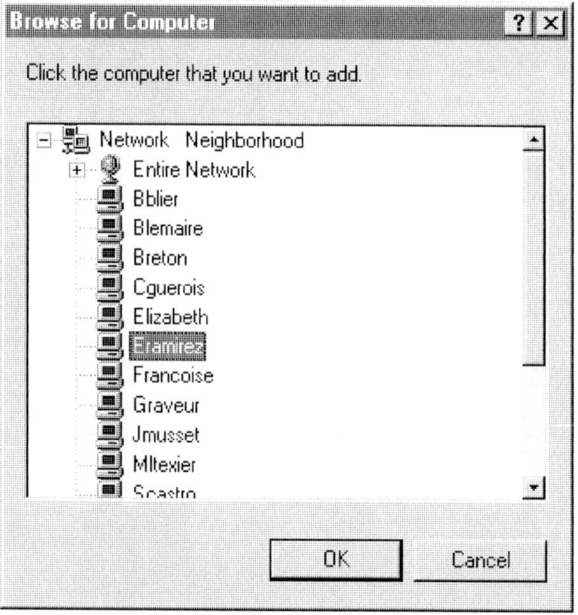

☞ Click **OK** to enter.

Defining the policy

After the preliminaries described above, you can assign a policy to a user, group or computer.

For example, you might want to prohibit the default user from editing the registry (REGEDIT.EXE) : either double-click the **Default User** (or) icon or go through **Edit - Properties** and apply a system restriction policy:

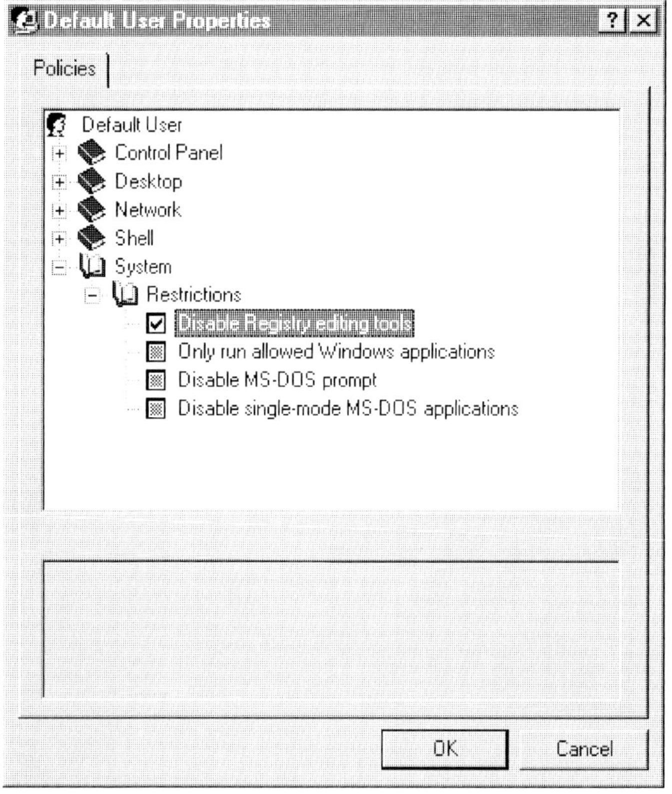

☞ Click **OK** to confirm.

Saving the policy

You should save the policy in a file named CONFIG.POL in the NETLOGON share of the NT domain controller, or in the Windows directory:

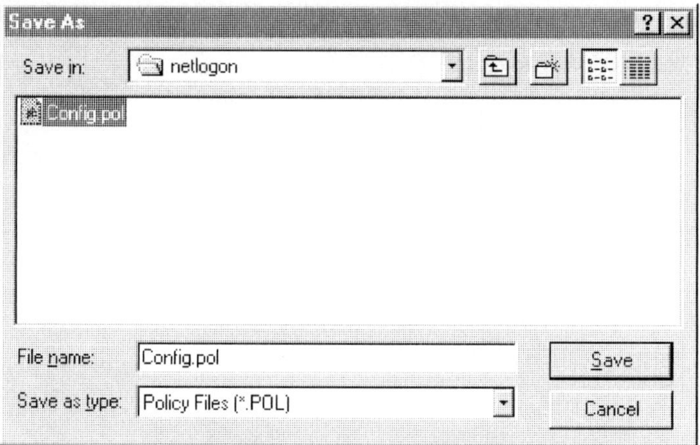

F. Connectivity with UNIX

The core version of Windows 95 includes an excellent implementation of TCP/IP along with two utilities which are widely exploited with UNIX: FTP and TELNET. These two utilities are installed automatically when the TCP/IP protocol suite is selected for a Windows 95 machine.

1. TELNET

TELNET (*Terminal EmuLation over the NETwork*) enables a Windows 95 machine to simulate a VT100 or ANSI terminal which is not connected by an asynchronous line, but by the local network.

Starting TELNET

☞ **Start**
Run

☞ Type TELNET.EXE at the command prompt.

If you often work with TELNET, you may find it worthwhile to create a shortcut on the desktop, or to add TELNET as an option to the **Start** menu.

Connecting to a remote TCP/IP machine

☞ **Connect**
Remote system

☞ Enter the IP address of the host you want to contact and, if necessary, enter the type of emulation you require:

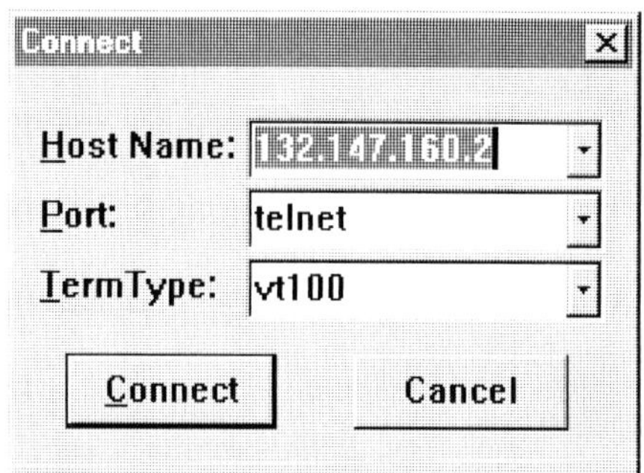

The remote UNIX host needs to have the TCP/IP protocol suite, of course. The TELNET daemon must also be running on this host:

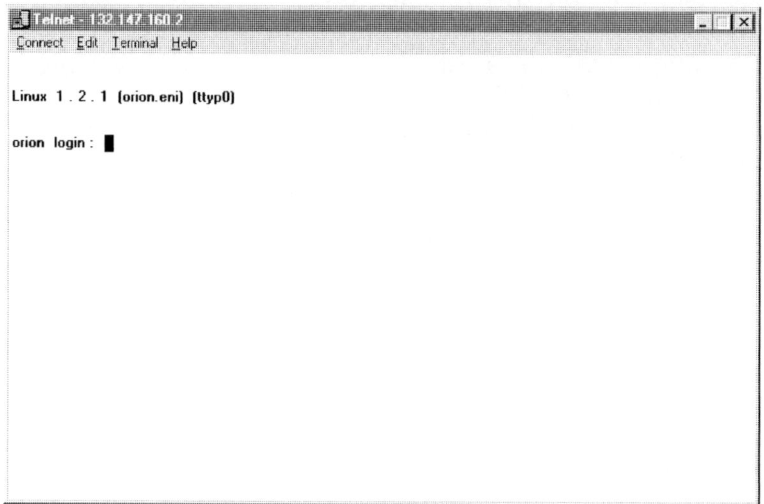

2. FTP

FTP *(File Transfer Protocol)* enables a Windows 95 machine to connect to a remote FTP server and to carry out a bi-directional file transfer.
It is a command line utility, and relies on the user's knowledge of the commands for opening a remote site, going into a local or remote directory and for receiving and sending files.

FTP commands

! *cmd_shell*	runs a local shell command.
Ascii	transfers in ASCII.
append *local_file* *remote_file*	adds a local file to the end of a file on the remote machine.
bell	sounds a beep at the end of each successful transfer.

binary	transfers a file in binary.
bye	end of FTP session and return to the shell.
cd	change directory on the remote machine.
close	ends a connection with a remote FTP server without leaving FTP.
debug	starts the debugger: commands sent to the remote machine are preceded by -->.
delete	deletes files on the remote machine.
dir *path*	displays the directory on the remote machine.
get *remote_file local_file*	copies a remote file into a local file.
glob	if glob is positioned, the expansion of wildcard characters is prohibited.
hash	if this indicator is positioned, display of the hash symbol is authorised during transfer.
help *command*	accesses FTP help.
lcd *local_directory*	changes directory on the local machine.
ls	displays the contents of the directory on the remote machine.
mdelete *remote_files*	deletes files from the remote machine.
mdir *remote_dirnames*	as dir, but several directory names can be given, separated by a space.
mget *remote_filenames*	transfers multiple files from the remote machine to the active directory on the local machine.
mkdir *dirname*	makes a new directory on the remote machine.
mls *remote_files*	as ls, but several names can be given, separated by spaces.
mput *local_files*	transfers multiple files from the local machine to the remote machine.
open *host/ip_address*	opens a session on a remote machine.

prompt	if this indicator is active (it is by default) the user has to give confirmation before deleting or transferring multiple files.
put *local_file remote_file*	copies a file from the local machine to the remote machine.
pwd	gives the current directory of the remote machine.
quit	ends the FTP session, returns to the shell.
quote	sends a command to the remote machine without performing it on the remote machine.
recv *remote_file local_file*	equivalent to get.
remotehelp *command*	accesses help relevant to the commands supported by the remote FTP server.
rename *old_name new_name*	renames a file or directory on the remote machine.
rmdir *dir_name*	deletes a directory on the remote machine.
send *local_file remote_file*	equivalent to put.
status	displays the current status of FTP.
type *ascii/binary*	specifies the type of transfer (ASCII or binary).
user *username*	identifies the user in relation to the remote machine's FTP server; a password may be required.
verbose	in verbose mode, all the remote FTP server's replies are displayed for the user and statistics are produced at the end of the transfer: this is the mode by default.

Example of an FTP session

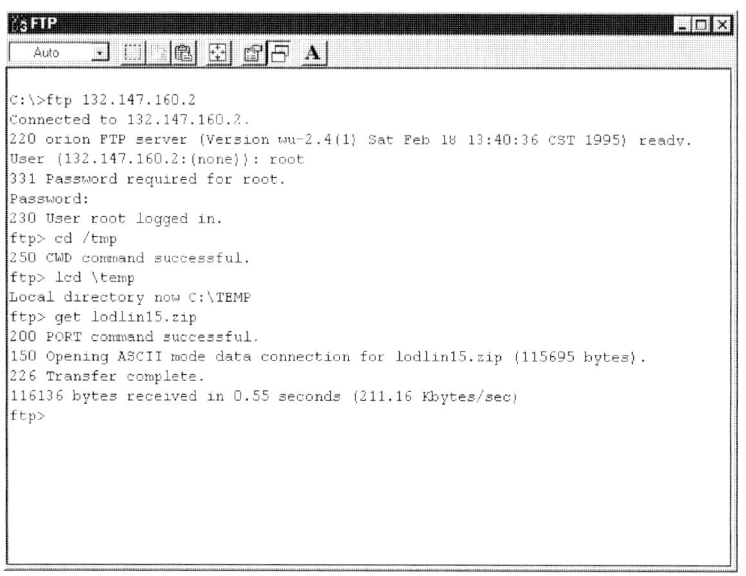
FTP
Auto
A
C:\>ftp 132.147.160.2
Connected to 132.147.160.2.
220 orion FTP server (Version wu-2.4(1) Sat Feb 18 13:40:36 CST 1995) ready.
User (132.147.160.2:(none)): root
331 Password required for root.
Password:
230 User root logged in.
ftp> cd /tmp
250 CWD command successful.
ftp> lcd \temp
Local directory now C:\TEMP
ftp> get lodlin15.zip
200 PORT command successful.
150 Opening ASCII mode data connection for lodlin15.zip (115695 bytes).
226 Transfer complete.
116136 bytes received in 0.55 seconds (211.16 Kbytes/sec)
ftp>

G. Interoperation with Novell NetWare

Windows 95 can be configured as either client or server in a NetWare network. Although several client services can run simultaneously under Windows 95, which means that the workstation can be a client in several networks at once (for example Microsoft and NetWare), it is not possible to run several server services at the same time. For this reason, a Windows 95 workstation cannot simultaneously be both a Microsoft network server and a NetWare network server.

The IPX/SPX protocol which is normally used in NetWare networks can use different types of frame:

- IEEE 802.2
- IEEE 802.3
- Ethernet II

The type of frame used can be defined manually or automatically. In the latter case, Windows 95 emits a message at startup which is coded in the different frame formats. It goes on to ignore the formats used for messages to which there is no reply.

1. Installing the client for NetWare networks

☞ Open the control panel or display the properties of the network neighbourhood by a right-click on Network Neighborhood .

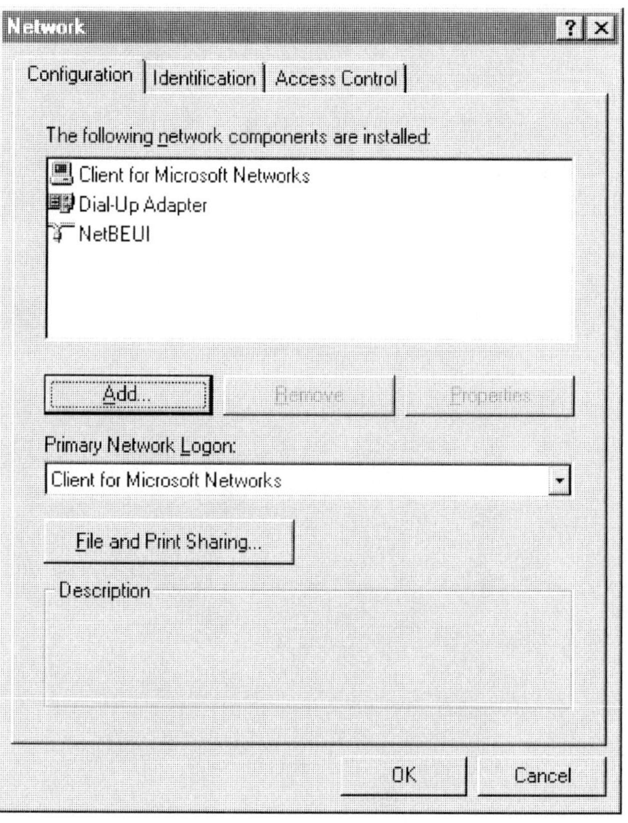

☞ Click the **Add** button:

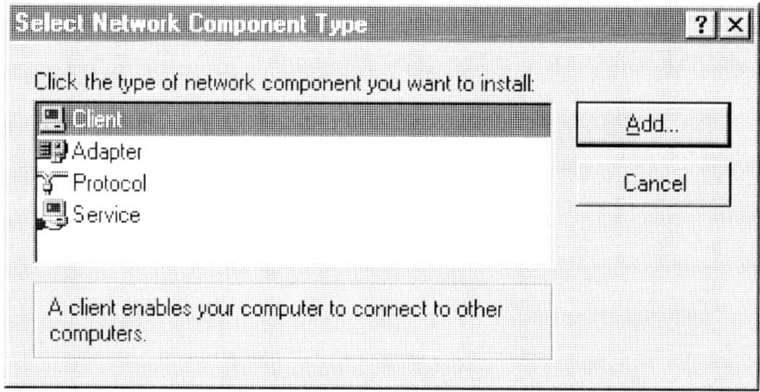

☞ In the list of components which can be added, chose **Client** then click **Add** again.

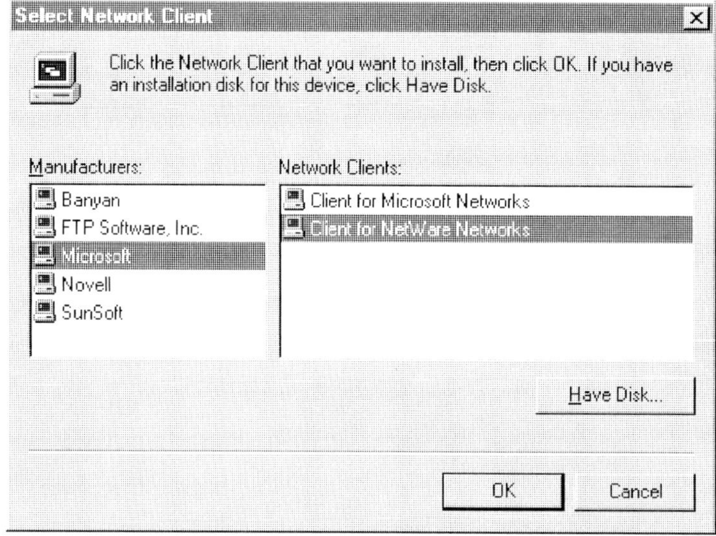

☞ Select the NetWare client supplied by Microsoft and click **OK** to confirm.

Settings for the IPX/SPX protocol

Once the installation phase is complete, you can edit the protocol's property and make certain changes:

☞ Select the protocol component in the list and click the **Properties** button.

Choosing the type of frame and the network number

Among others, these two settings can be modified on the **Advanced** properties page:

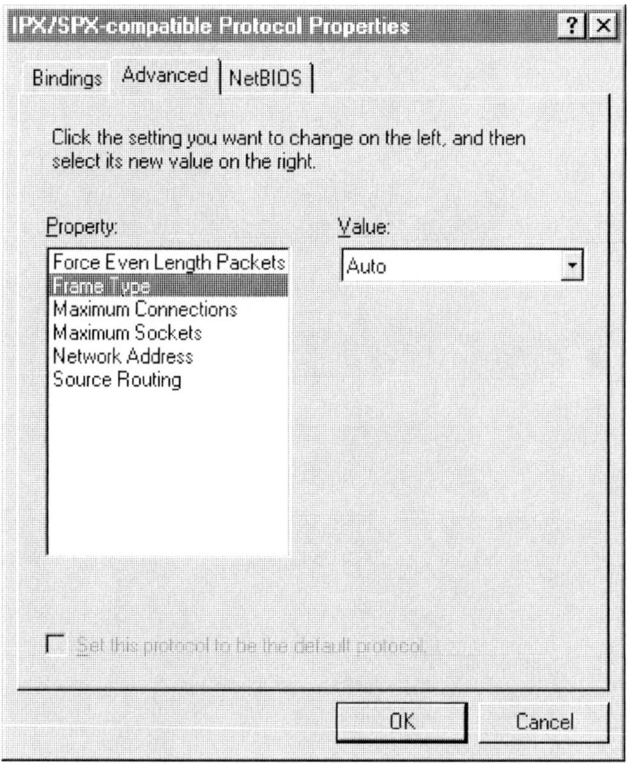

*If you are using several protocols, the **default protocol** check box becomes available after you have restarted the computer. This is an important option which enables one protocol to take precedence over the others. It is a good idea to select the protocol most exploited on the workstation and activate this check box for it.*

Determining whether or not to use NetBIOS over IPX

If you intend to use applications which make use of NetBIOS over the IPX protocol, activate the check box available in the protocol's properties:

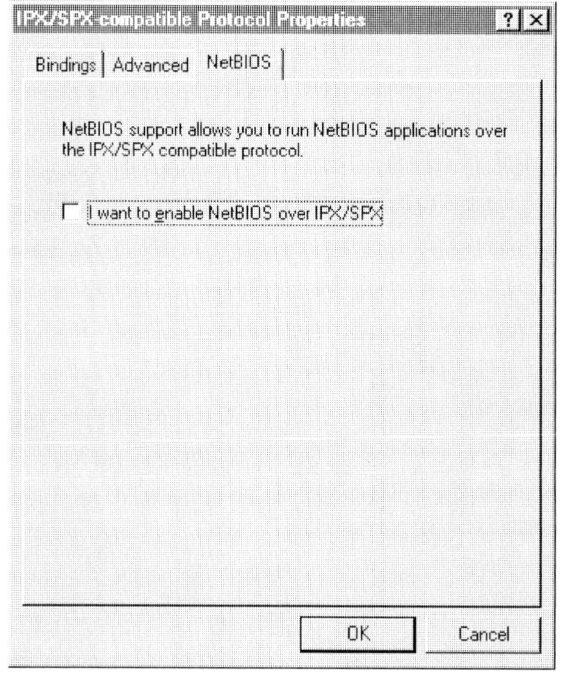

Binding the protocol to different network clients

This property of the protocol can make a difference to the workstation's performance if several clients are installed. If, for example, you use IPX/SPX exclusively for communicating with a NetWare server, and all your communications with the Microsoft server are carried by a different protocol (NetBEUI or TCP/IP), you should consider deactivating the IPX binding for the Microsoft client.

This would improve the network performance of the workstation:

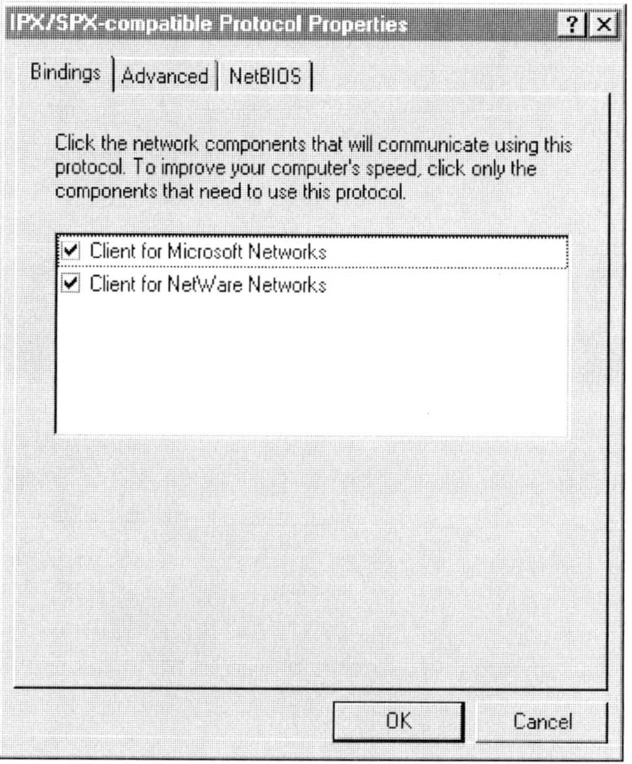

NetWare client settings

At the end of the client installation procedure, after any changes to the protocol parameters, Windows 95 prompts you to restart the workstation:

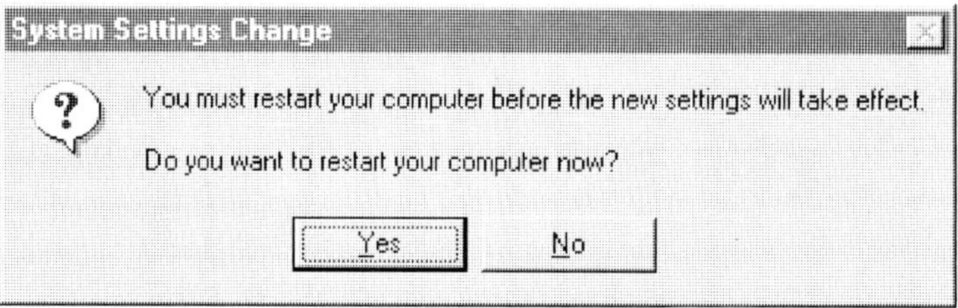

Once you have done this, you need to configure the NetWare client, if only to indicate which is the preferred server and whether or not the connection script should be processed. This information is includes in the properties of the NetWare client:

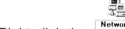

- Right-click the  icon and choose **Properties**.
- In the list of network components, select **Client for NetWare Networks** then click the **Properties** button.

☞ Select the preferred server for NetWare and click **OK**.

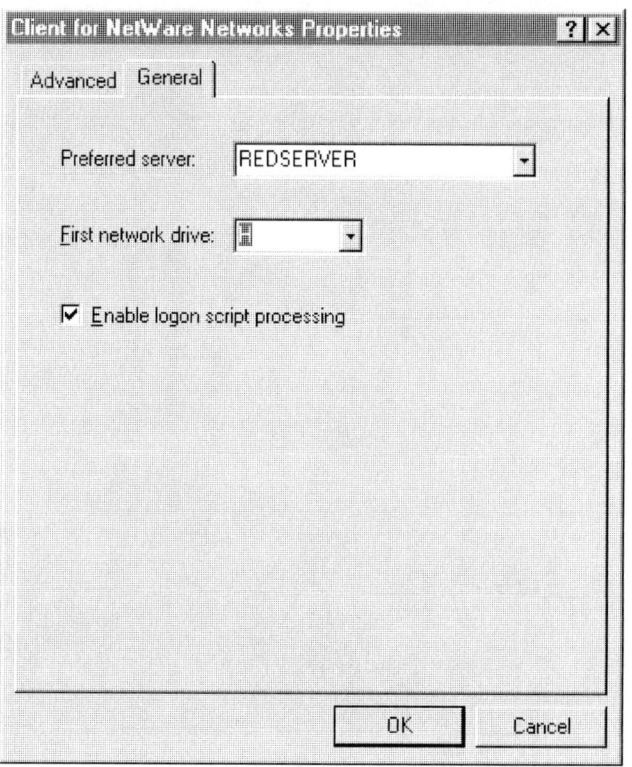

Exploiting the capacities of the NetWare client

The NetWare client is transparent: when you browse the network in the Explorer, there is nothing to distinguish NetWare resources from other resources. The procedure for mapping a network drive is the same whether the drive corresponds to a NetWare resource or a Microsoft resource:

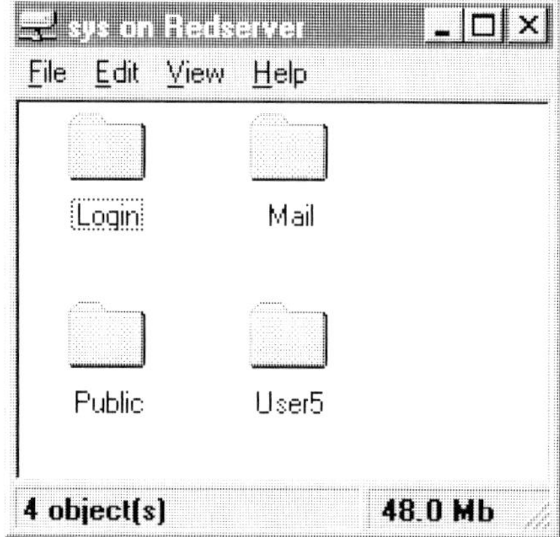

The shortcut menu which appears when you right-click the Network Neighborhood icon contains an additional option, **Who Am I**, which displays the preferred server and the name to which it is mapped:

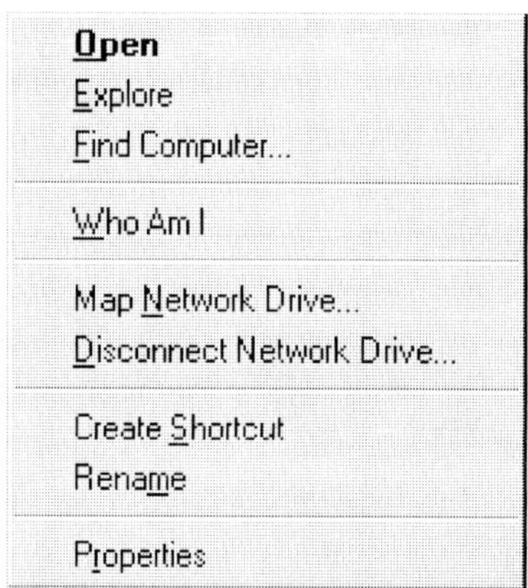

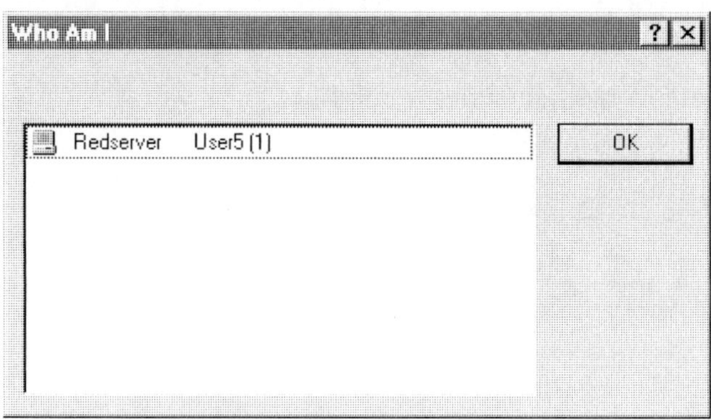

2. Installing the server service for NetWare networks

If the resource sharing service for Microsoft is installed, you must remove it before installing the sharing service for NetWare networks.

Once you have, if necessary, uninstalled the server service for Microsoft, go through the following procedure:

- Display the properties of the network neighbourhood by a right-click on .

- Click the **Add** button.

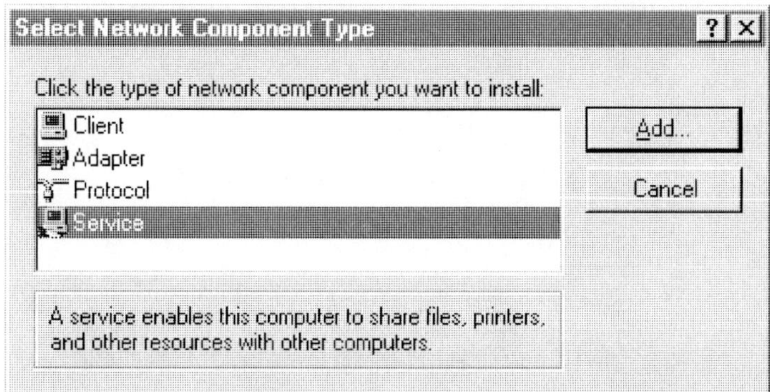

☞ In the list of available components, choose **Service** then click **Add** again.

☞ Next select the service **File and printer sharing for NetWare networks**.

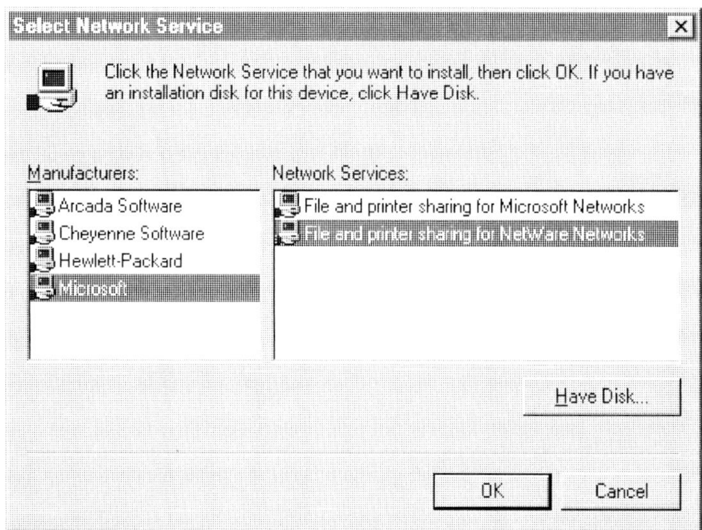

☞ Click **OK** twice to confirm.

Restart the workstation, following the system prompt:

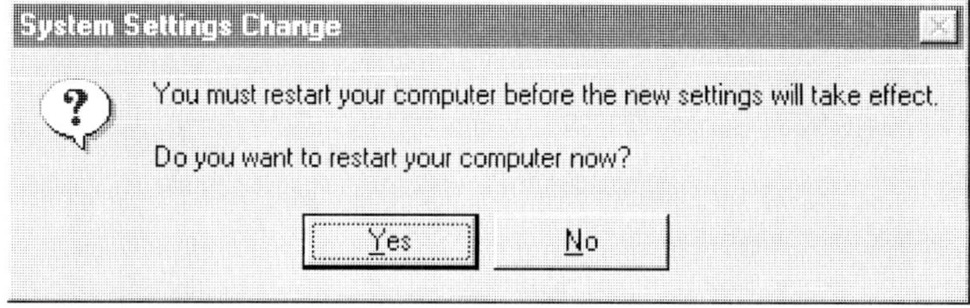

If you want to use the file and printer sharing service in a NetWare network, you must apply user-level security: the list of user accounts must be obtained from a veritable NetWare server:

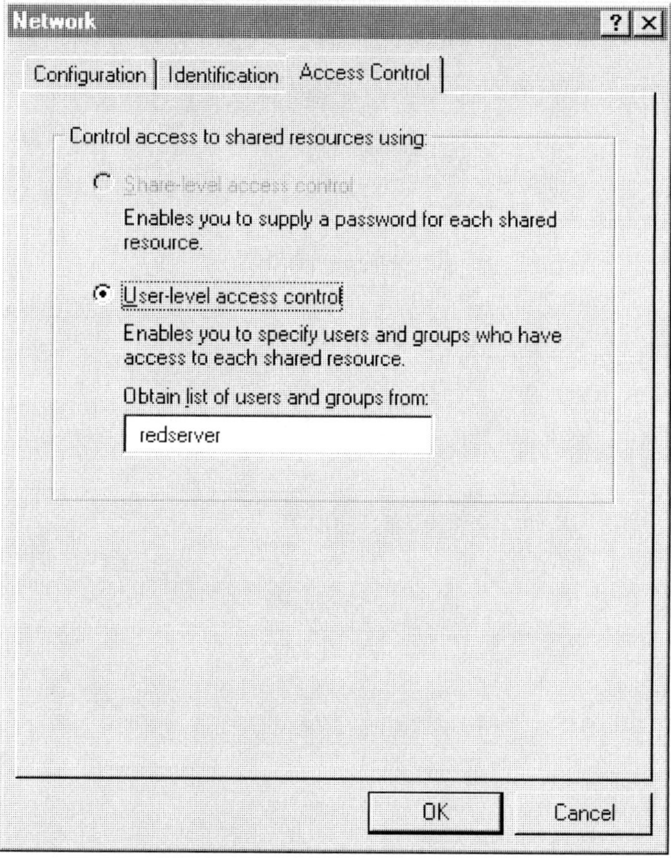

Once you have this list, you can share the resource by giving permissions (Read-Only, Full Access or Custom) to one of the users included in the *bindery*:

H. Remote access to the network

1. Overview

The remote access service enables a Windows 95 workstation equipped with a modem to make a remote connection to a network, which may be a workgroup or a domain. The user of the workstation can work in the remote network as if it were his/her own, except for a difference in the speed of operations, which is limited to the speed of the modem transmission.

All the network protocols supplied by Microsoft are supported:

- TCP/IP
- NetBEUI
- IPX/SPX

A Windows 95 machine can act as remote access **client** or remote access **server**.

2. Configuring the remote access client

☞ To make a connection, go via the **Start** menu:

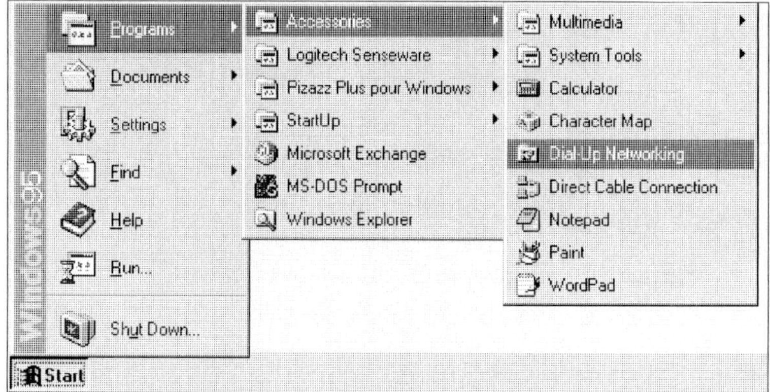

The Dial-Up Networking window appears:

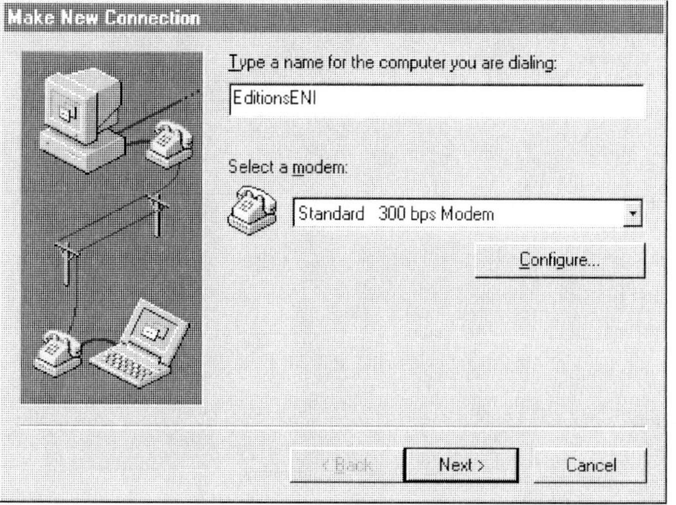

☞ Click the **Next** button.
The first step is to give a name for the new remote connection and to select a modem:

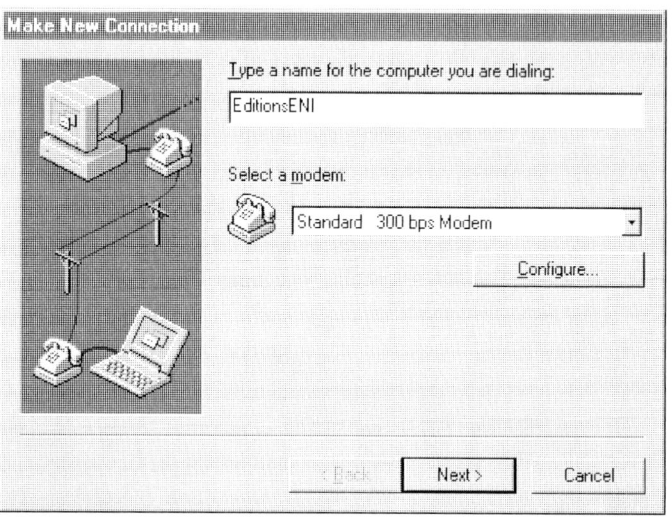

☞ Fill in the information then click **Next**.

Give the number to call and the country code:

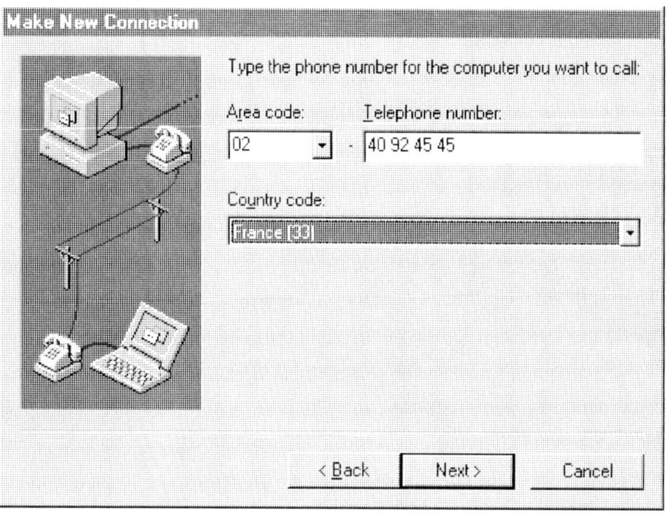

☞ Click the **Next** button.

☞ To complete the installation, click :

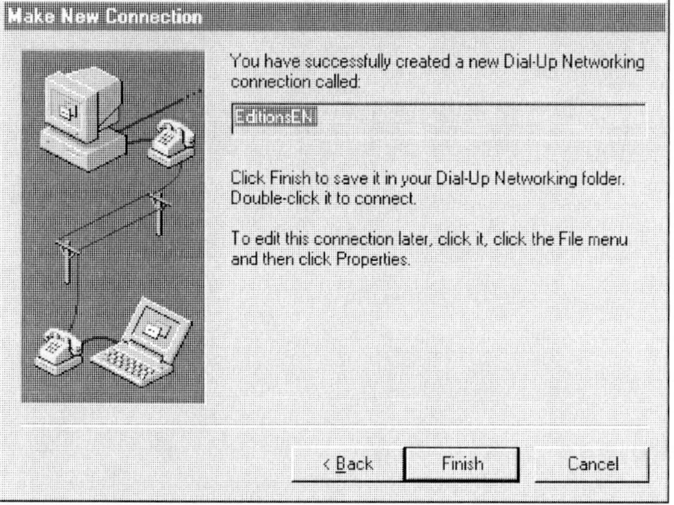

If the dial-up adapter has not yet been installed, or if it has been removed, the following message is displayed:

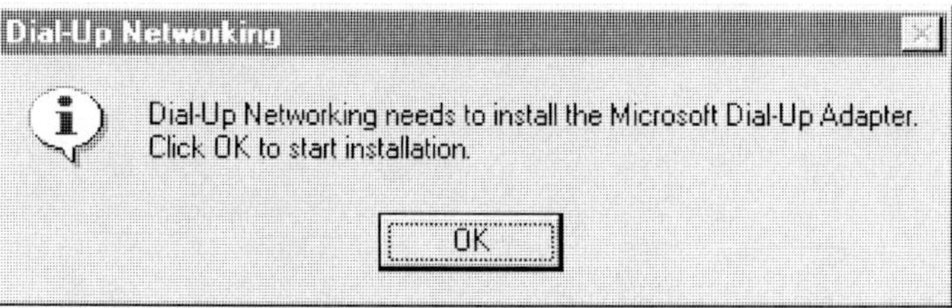

☞ Click **OK** to go ahead with the installation.

To dial the telephone number and connect to the network via the modem, all you need to do is double-click the new connection or open the **Connections** menu and take the **Connect** option.

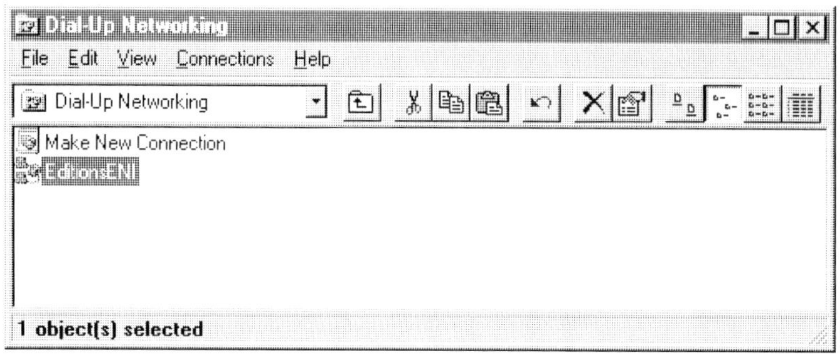

3. Configuring the remote access server

You can only configure your machine as a remote access server if you have acquired and installed the Microsoft Plus! CD-ROM and if you have a modem which is correctly installed.

- Open 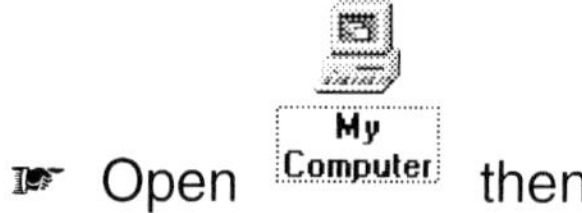 then

- **Connections**
  Dial-up server...
  This option is only available if Microsoft Plus! has been installed.

- Activate the **Allow caller access** then make the access secure with a password.

You can click the **Server Type** button to determine the type of the server.

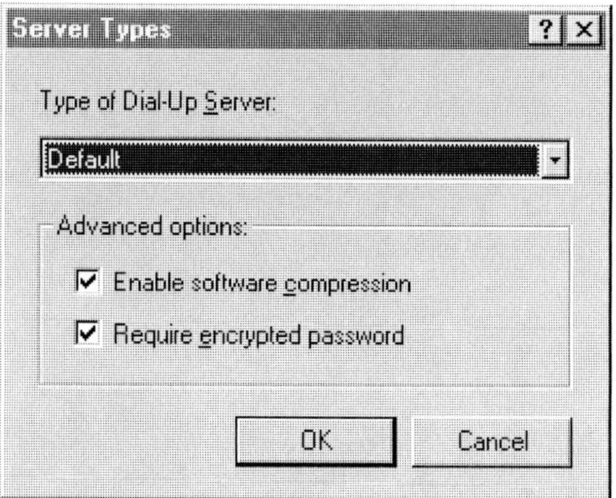

You have the choice between a server which uses the PPP protocol (like NT Server 3.5 or UNIX) or a server which uses ASYBEUI (like NT advanced Server 3.1 or Windows for Workgroups). In this same window, there are also options for compression and encryption.

☞ Validate the whole set of options by clicking **OK**.

The automatic Fax response is not operational if you are using dial-up networking.

↓personal notes↓

Microsoft Exchange

A. General remarks

Just as NetBIOS gives applications independence from the transport used, MAPI (*Messaging Application Interface*) allows applications to use a set of API functions to communicate, independently of the way in which the message is transported (Fax, Internet mail service, CompuServe...). MAPI also provides OLE interfaces.

In the search for a general mail API, MAPI, which existed already in earlier versions of Windows, is the solution that Microsoft proposes.

In direct contact with this programming interface, Microsoft Exchange is the successor to MSMail, the earliest versions of which were supplied with Windows for Workgroups. It greatly improves on these versions, however, and is now an extremely efficient application which manages all aspects of sending and receiving messages , whatever the network used for transmission (LAN, WAN, fax...).

B. Installing Microsoft Exchange

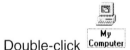

☞ Double-click 

then 

.

☞ Select the **Windows Setup** tab then activate **Microsoft Exchange** in the list:

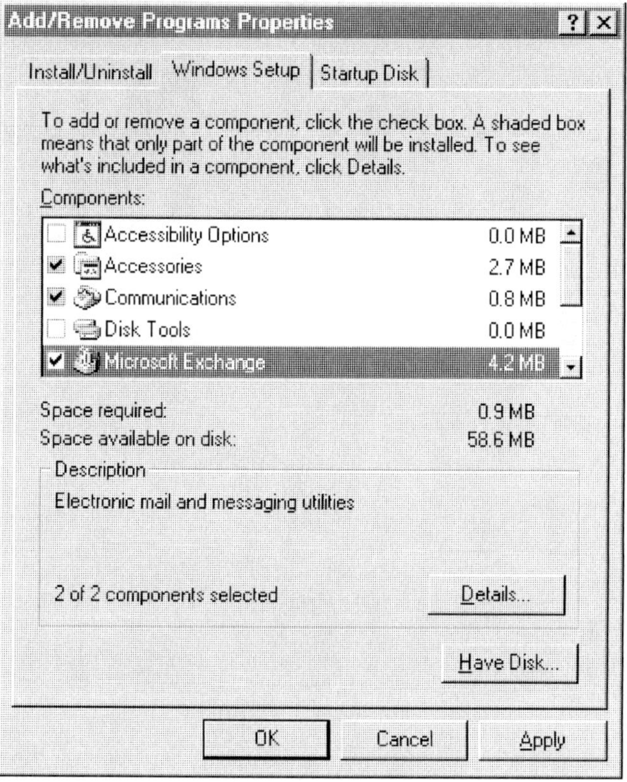

☞ Click **OK**.

The **Inbox Setup Wizard** starts:

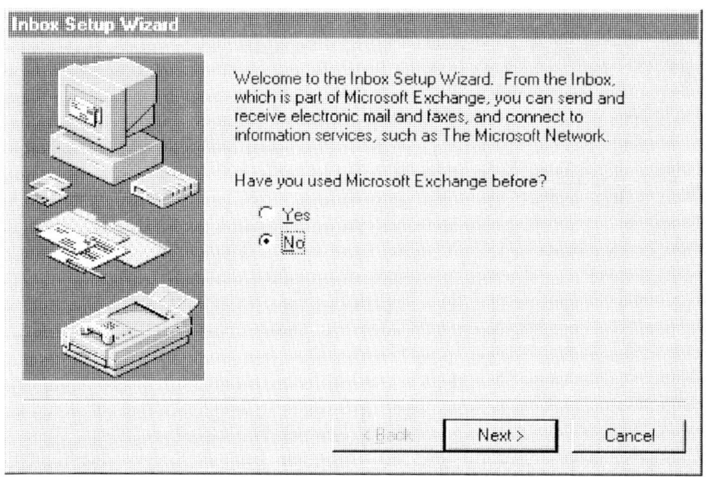

☞ Click the **Next** button to continue.

Various delivery services can be used for transmitting messages. The first step is to select the services which correspond to the components installed. Three send/receive services are proposed:

– Fax
– Mail
– Internet

☞ Activate the services you require.

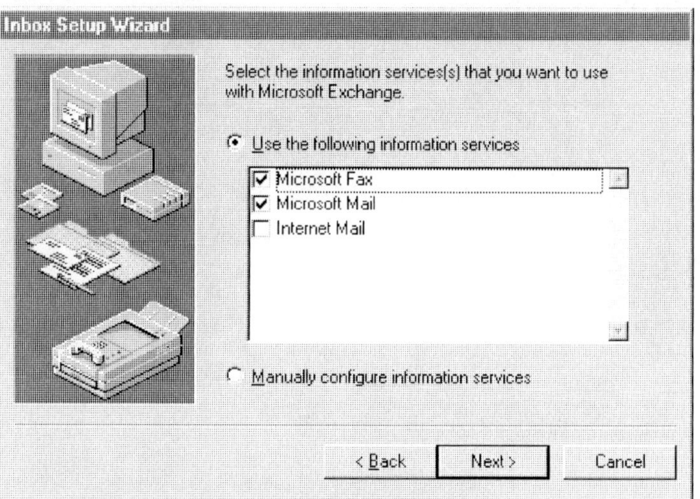

☞ Click **Next**.

If you have selected the fax service, you need to indicate the type of modem you are using. Either select or create the fax modem:

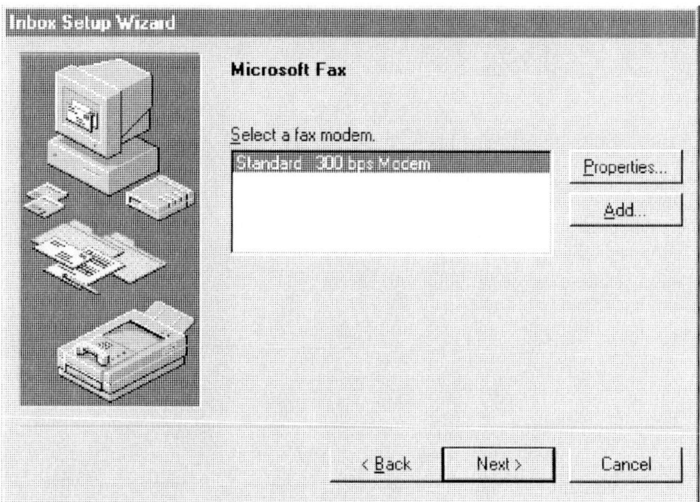

☞ Click the **Next** button to continue.

At this point you have to indicate whether or not Windows 95 should automatically answer each call on the line to which the modem is connected. This depends on whether or not the telephone line is dedicated to the fax.

The value of this option can be modified at a later date. There is also a third possible value which has Windows 95 inform you immediately of an incoming call so that you can decide whether or not to authorise reception of a fax. This solution is advantageous if your telephone line is used both for vocal communication and for the fax (see the section on *Configuring the fax service* later on in this chapter).

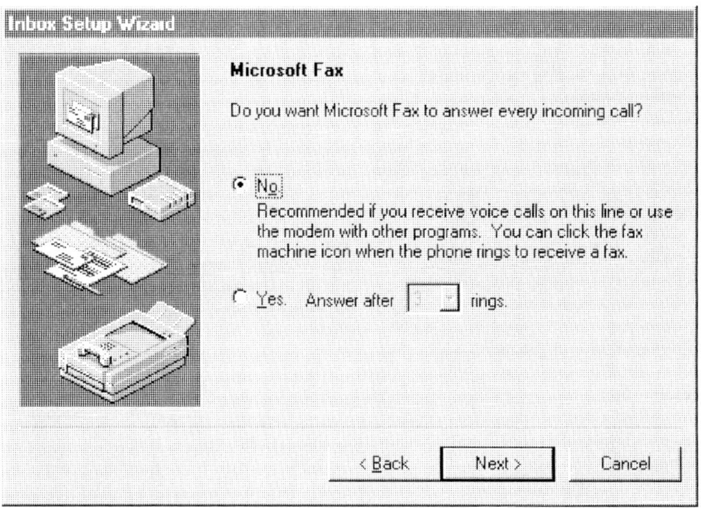

☞ Click the **Next** button again.

The Wizard asks for your name and local fax number.

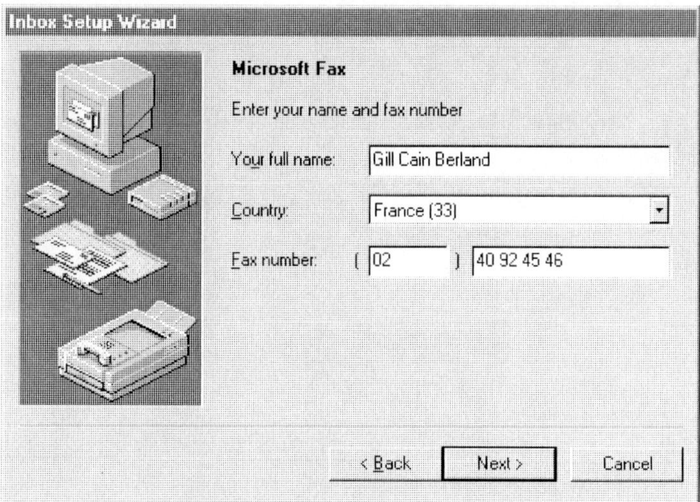

☞ Fill in the information and press **Next**.

The next question requires a precise answer: the location of the hierarchy which makes up the postoffice.

One of the following circumstances applies:

- The postoffice already exists. In this case, enter its UNC path into the dialog box.
- The postoffice does not exist yet. In this case, you must create it. But how can you do this when you have not finished installing Microsoft Mail ?

☞ Use the **Start** menu to open the control panel, then double-click 

.

☞ Follow the procedure described in the section on *Creating a postoffice* in this chapter.

☞ When you have created the postoffice, return to installing exchange and supply the UNC path:

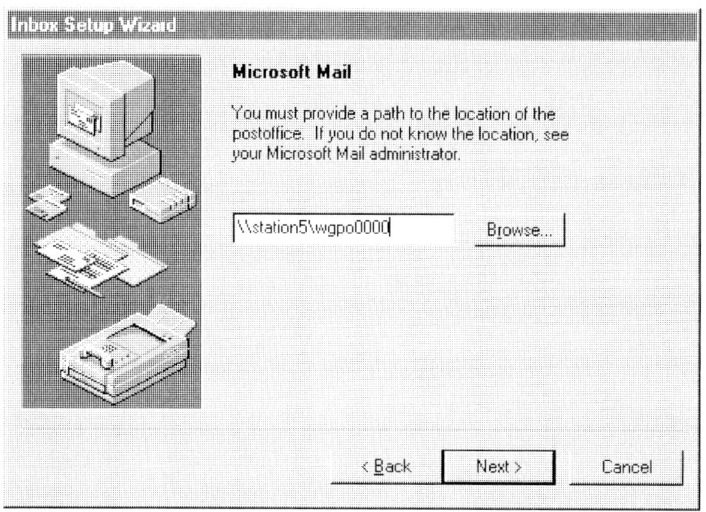

☞ Click the **Next** button.

☞ Select your name from the list of people who have access to the postoffice (you will have created your postoffice account when you created the postoffice) then give your password.

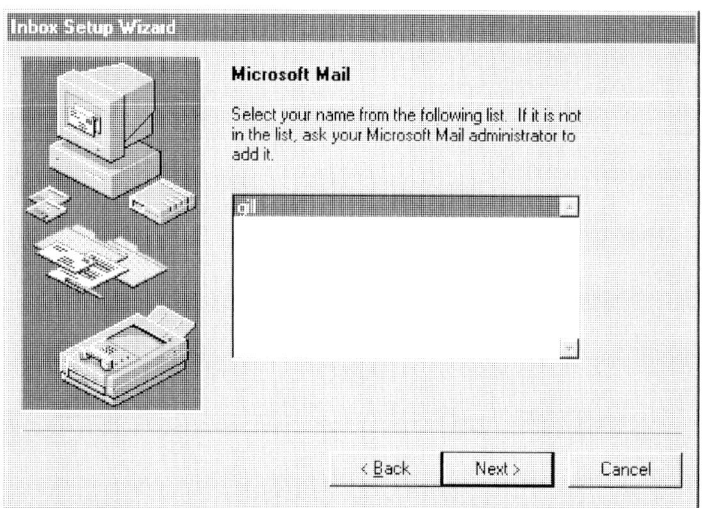

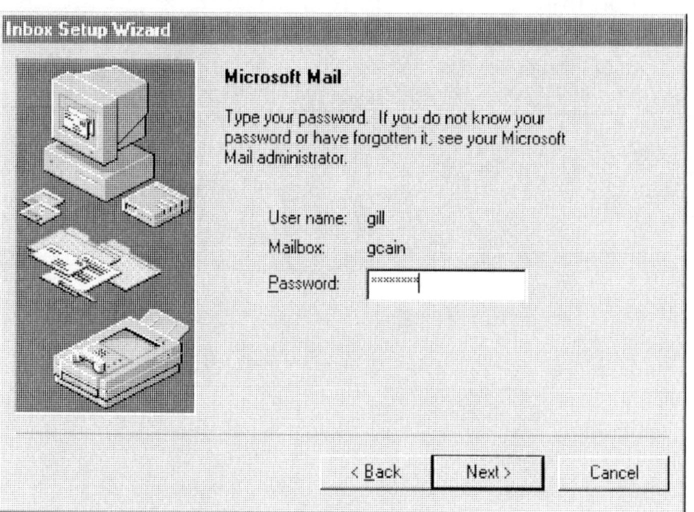

If you intend Windows to receive faxes automatically on a permanent basis, it is *indispensable* to open the inbox automatically at system startup. If not, you can start Exchange when you need it.

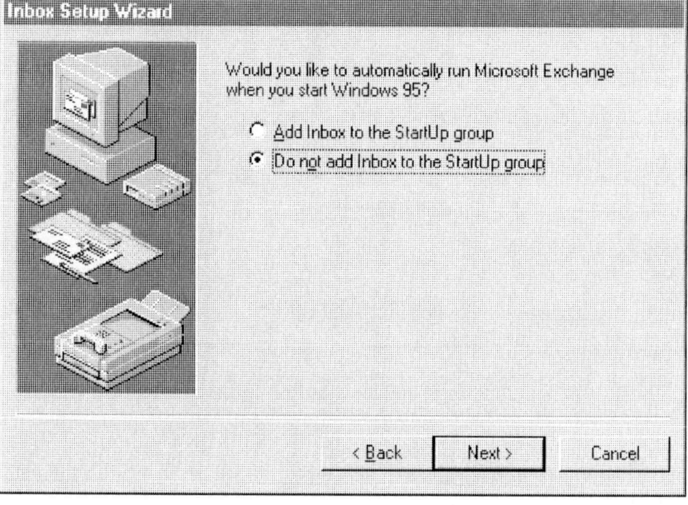

☞ Activate the appropriate option button then go on to the next step:

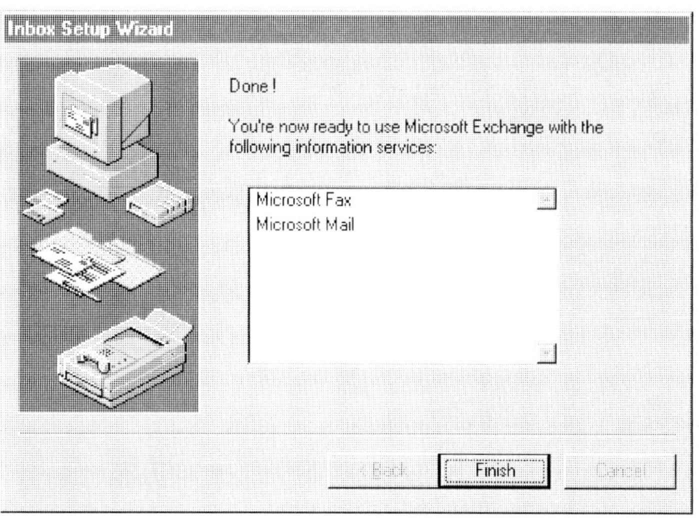

☞ Click the **Finish** button.

A new icon appears on the desktop. It represents the inbox  .

C. Creating a postoffice

This is a simple operation, but essential for operating Microsoft Exchange. It determines the physical location of the postoffice hierarchy, the names of postoffice users and other information concerning them.

The routing of mail between different postoffices is not performed by this version of the application (use Mail Server for this function). As a rule, then, there should only be one postoffice.

To create a postoffice, proceed as follows:

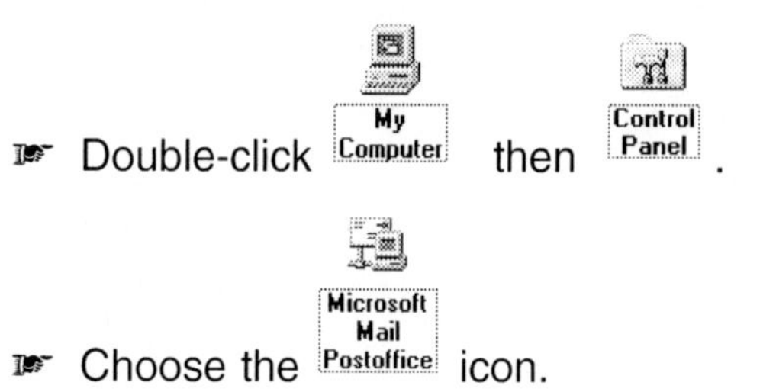

☞ Double-click My Computer then Control Panel.

☞ Choose the Microsoft Mail Postoffice icon.

In the **Postoffice Admin** dialog box, you can choose either to administer an existing postoffice, or to create a new one.

☞ Select **Create** then click the **Next** button.

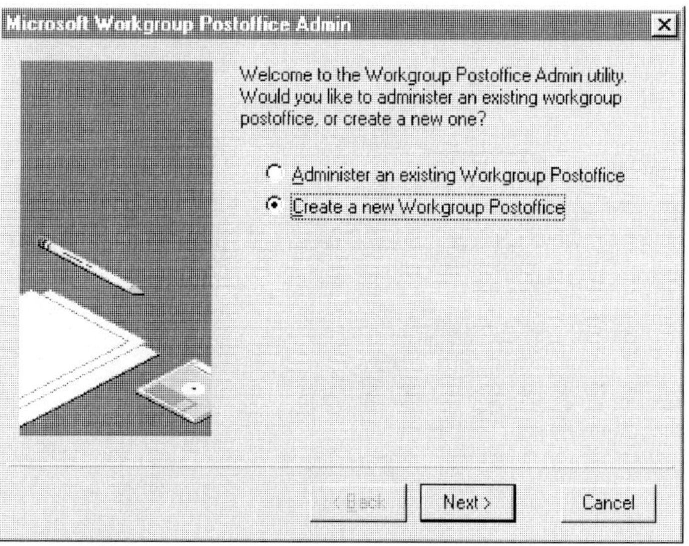

☞ Give the location you intend for the postoffice: the path could be a UNC path or one which corresponds to a local disk:

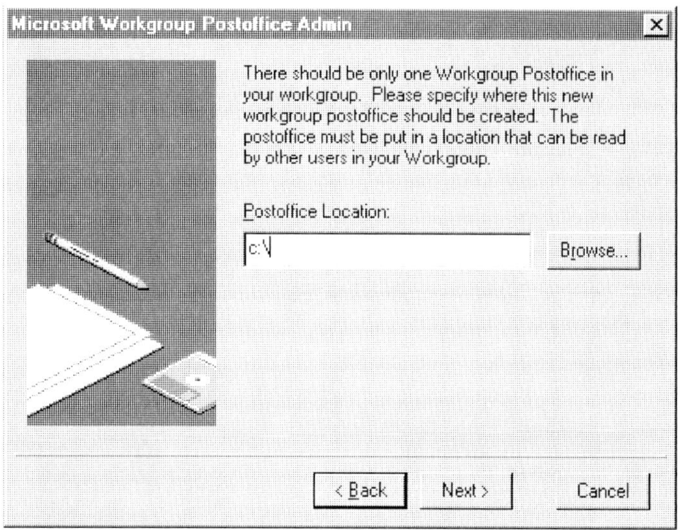

☞ Click the **Next** button.

☞ A click on the **Next** button confirms the creation of a postoffice, which is a directory named WGPxxxx, where xxxx is a four-digit number:

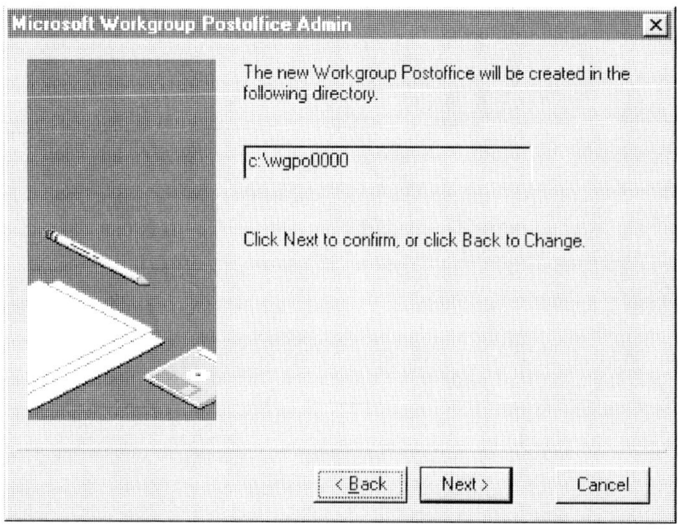

☞ Next give details of at least one user, the postoffice administrator. Only the first two text boxes in the dialog box are obligatory: the user name and the mailbox:

Enter Your Administrator Account Details

Name: Gill
Mailbox: gcain
Password: PASSWORD
Phone #1: 40 92 45 45
Phone #2:
Office:
Department: Editiorial
Notes:

OK Cancel

☞ Click **OK** to validate the data entered.

The postoffice must be shared with *full access* rights: a dialog box appears to remind you:

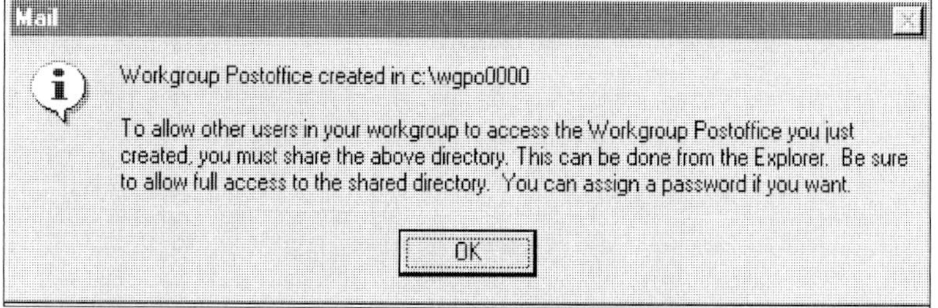

☞ In the Explorer, select the WGPO0000 directory, right-click it and take the **Sharing** option to share the postoffice, authorising **Full Access**.

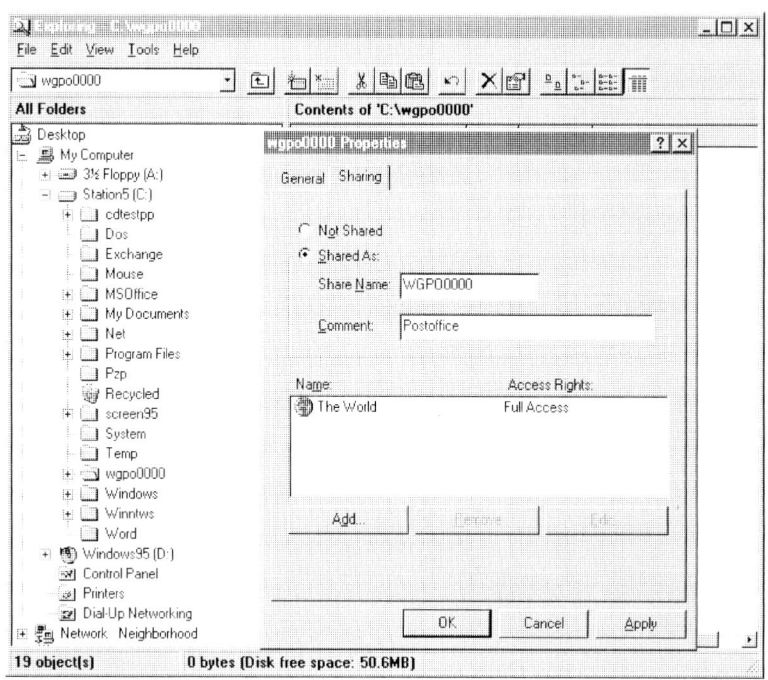

The postoffice is ready for use.

D. Administering an existing postoffice

Administering a postoffice consists mainly of creating user accounts as they are required:

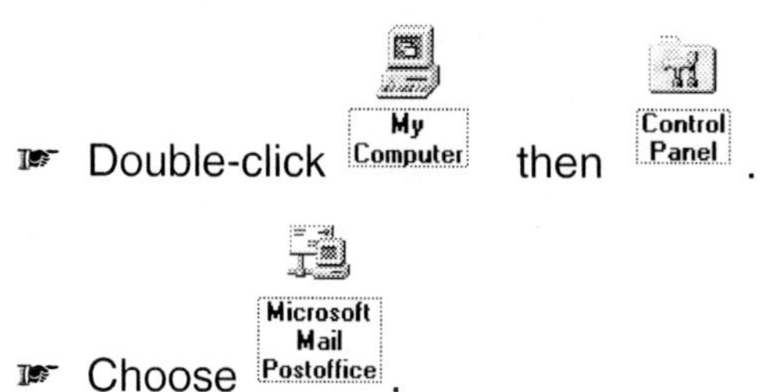

☞ Double-click My Computer then Control Panel.

☞ Choose Microsoft Mail Postoffice.

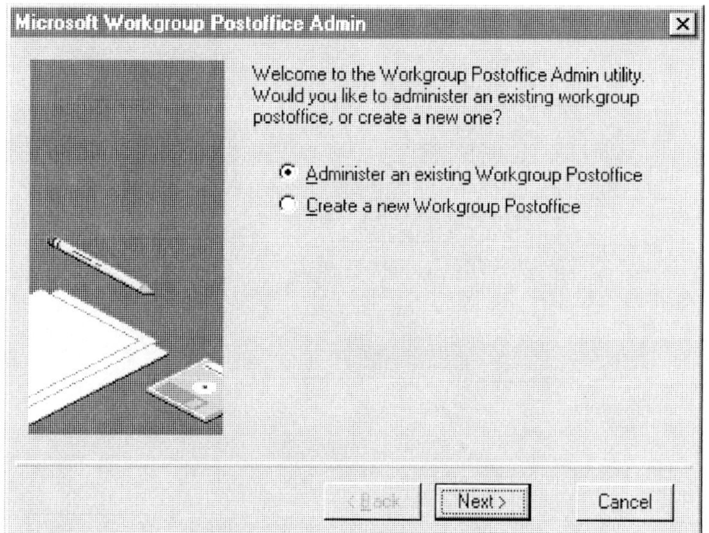

☞ Choose **Administer an existing workgroup postoffice** then click the **Next** button.

- If necessary, modify the path to the postoffice, or confirm the proposed path, which is normally correct, by clicking **Next**.

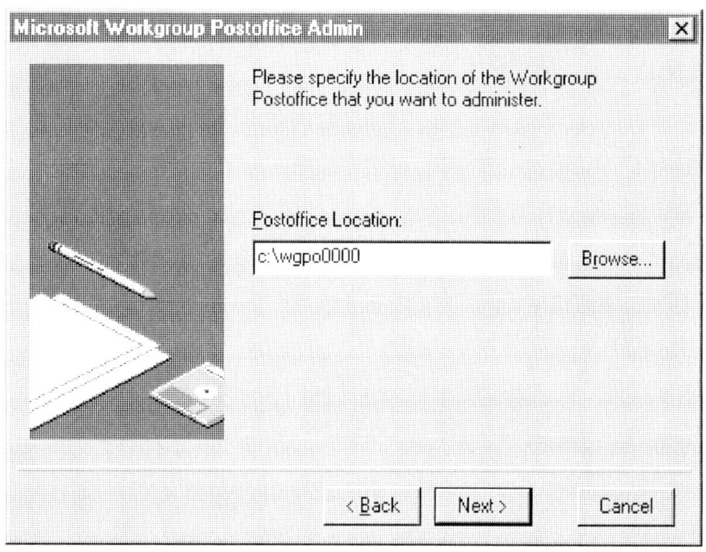

- Give your name and password to identify yourself as administrator of the postoffice:

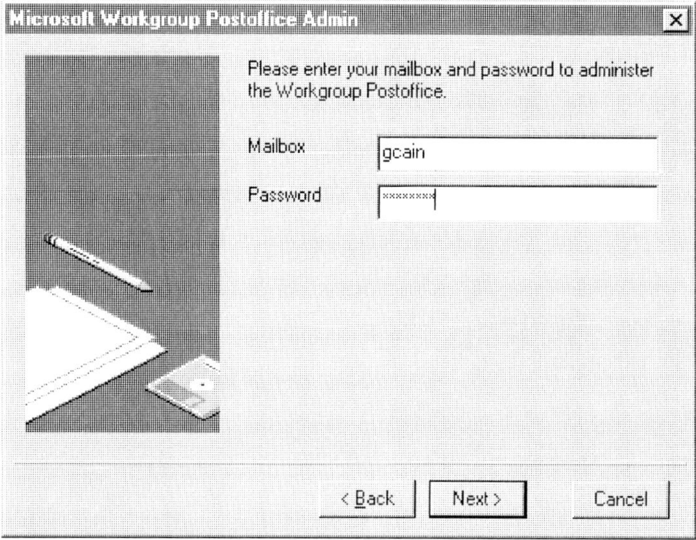

☞ Go on to the next stage where you can create postoffice users and modify the data concerning existing users by clicking the **Add User** and **Details** buttons.

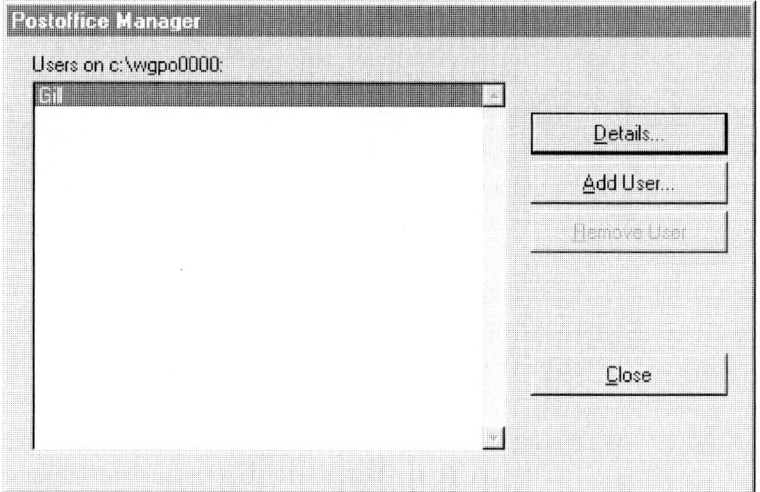

E. Using Microsoft Exchange

1. Reading a message

The first thing you need to do before you can read a new message is to double-click the **Inbox** (unless, of course, the inbox is included in the **Startup** group of the **Start** menu).

New messages are represented by a line which starts with a yellow envelope, to indicate that the message has not yet been read:

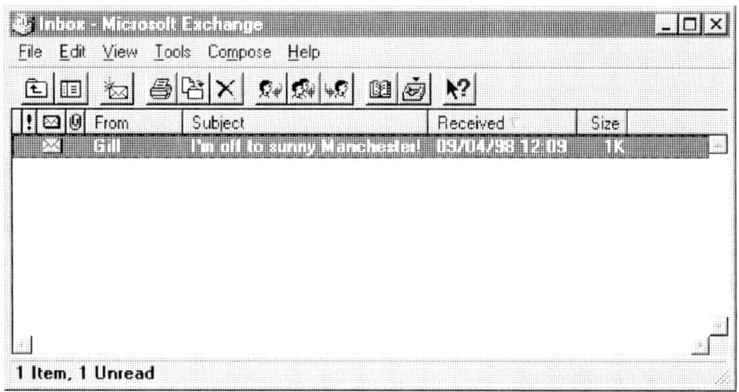

To read the message, double click the line. The contents appear:

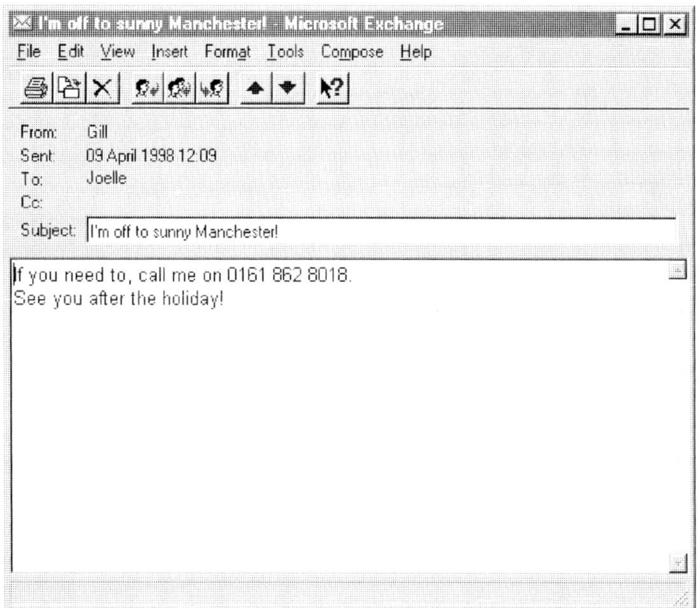

Once you have read the message, you can delete it. This involves moving it to the **Deleted Items** folder. The message is only permanently deleted when you leave the inbox.

To delete a message:

☞ **File**
Delete

To move up to the level above in the Exchange hierarchy, so that you can see all the folders:

☞ **View**
Folders

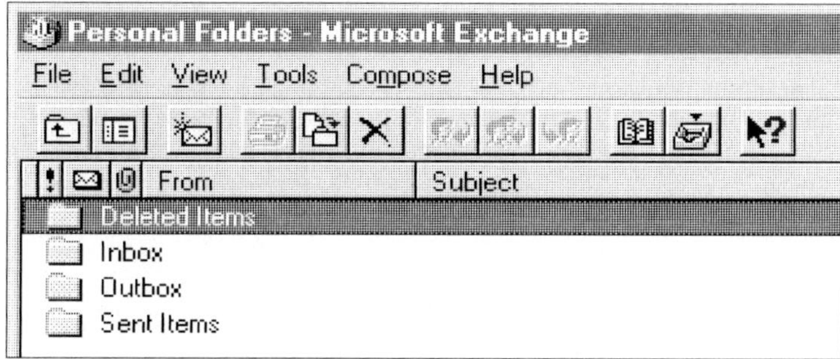

2. Sending a message

The procedure for sending a message is as follows:

☞ Double-click 

to open the inbox.

☞ **Compose**
New Message

Microsoft Exchange

The **New Message** window appears:

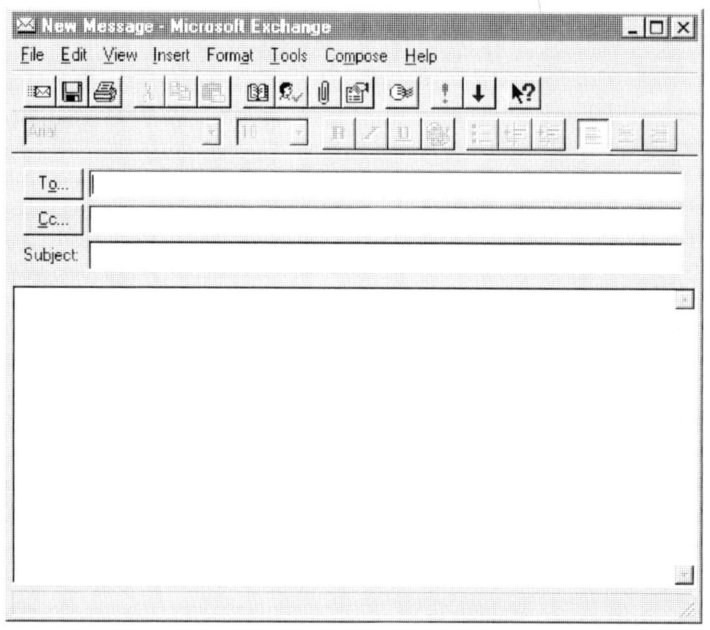

The first step is to indicate, in the **To...** field, the intended receiver of the message.

☞ You can type in the name manually, or you can click to open the address book:

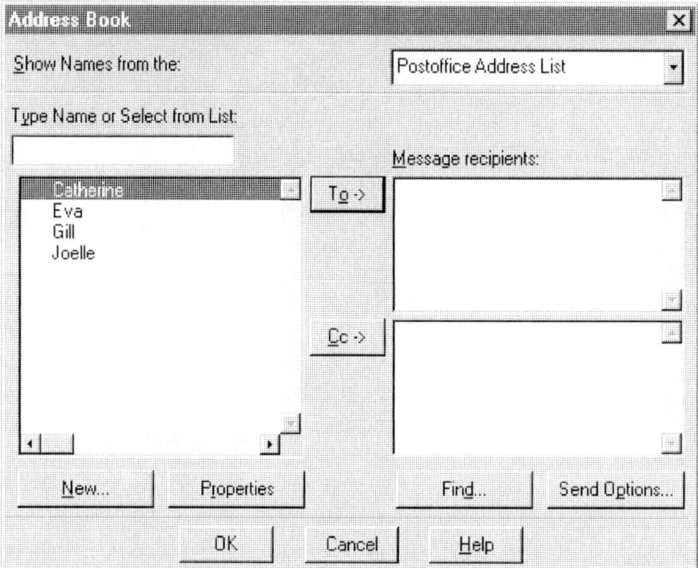

The address book contains the list of all the users of the postoffice.

☞ Select the recipient(s) of the message by clicking A ->. When you have finished selecting, click **OK** to confirm.

☞ If you select a user by clicking the Cc... button, he/she will receive a "carbon copy" of the message.

If you wish, give the message a descriptive title in the **Subject** field, then enter the body of the message itself.
In the message's property sheet, displayed by a click on , you have access to additional options: you can set the message's priority level, or ensure that you receive a delivery receipt or a read receipt for the message.

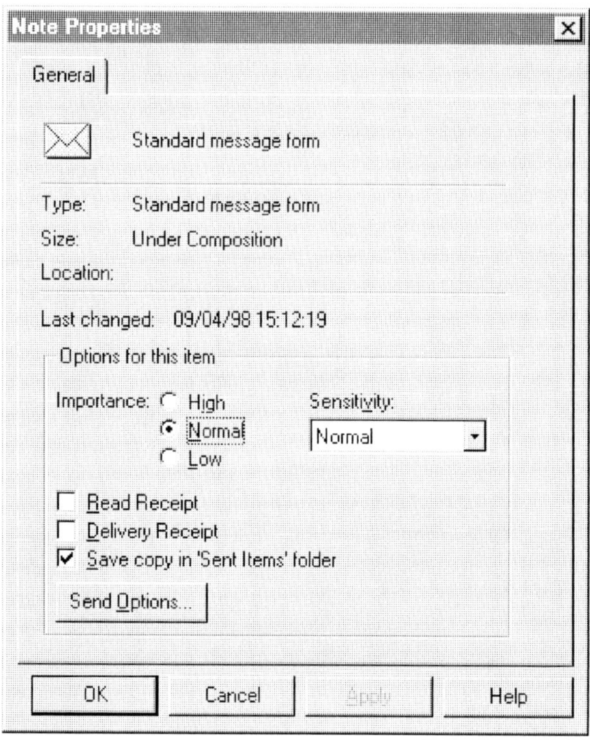

When you are ready to send the message:

 **File**
Send

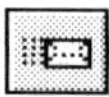

3. Receiving a fax

Exchange receives a fax either automatically or manually, depending on the configuration options set for the fax service.

For reception of faxes to be possible, the inbox must be open and the remote access server service must be deactivated.

A fax which has been received appears as a message in the inbox and can be read by a double-click. Only the icon distinguishes it from a mail message:

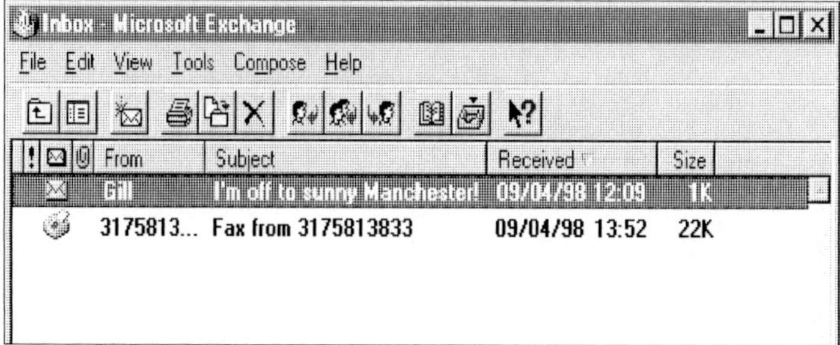

You can display and print the fax in the fax viewer, or edit it.

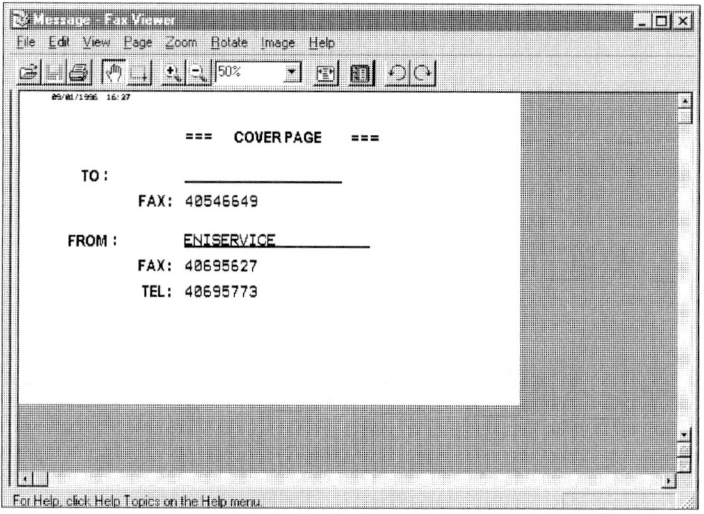

4. Sending a fax

There are different ways of sending a fax. Windows 95 considers the fax modem as a printer. You can print a document from the application which created it and direct it to the fax.

Another method is to open the **Compose** menu in the **Inbox** window and to take the **New Fax** option:

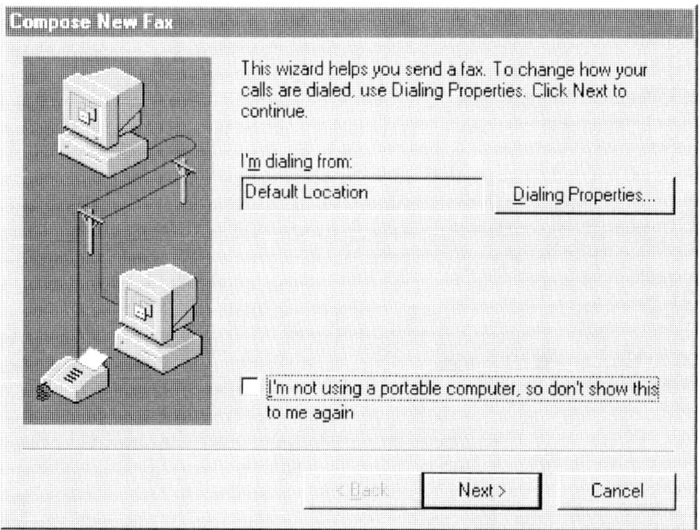

- If you are not using a portable computer, click the check box so that you will not need to give your co-ordinates again (of course, from a portable, you do need to say where you are calling from each time you send a fax) and click **Next**.
- Give details of the fax's recipient, name and fax number: if you prefer, you can select this information from the personal address book.

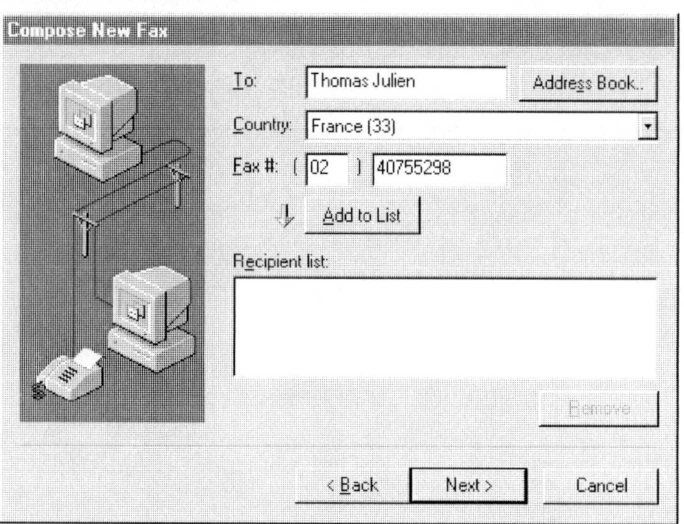

☞ Click the **Add to List** button to confirm the information you have entered, then click **Next**.

☞ If you require a cover page, choose one from the four standard cover pages provided:
Confidential!
Generic
For your information
Urgent !

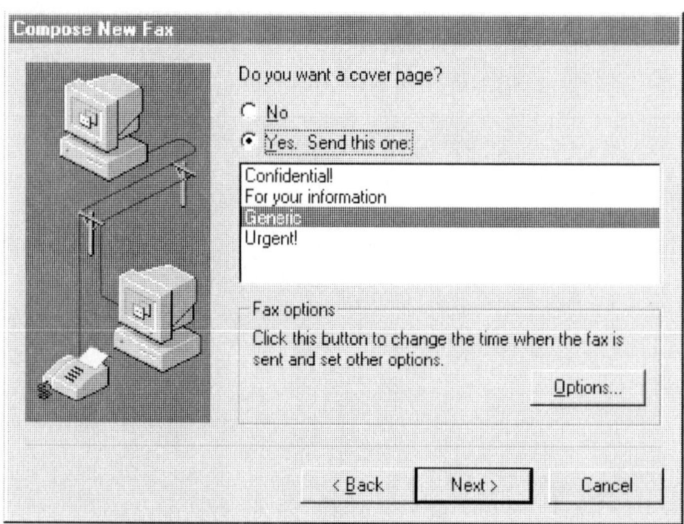

You can use the Cover Page Editor, included in the core version of Windows 95 to make changes to the built-in pages or to create new ones.

☞ Confirm your choice of cover page by clicking the **Next** button.

☞ The next step is to specify the subject of the message and the text:

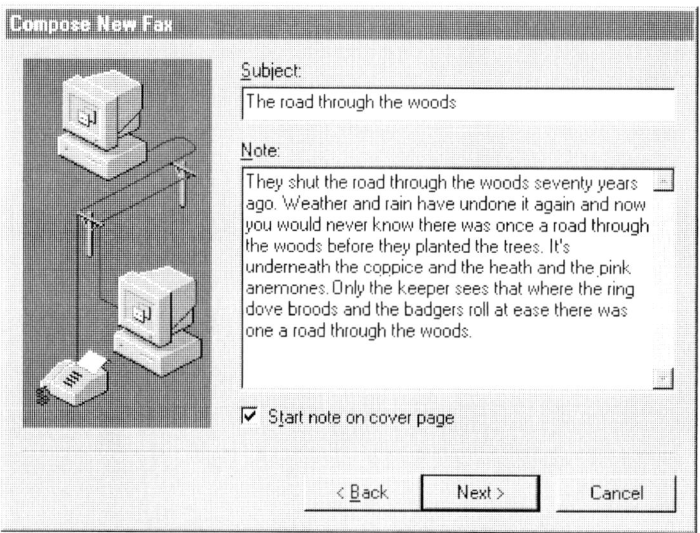

☞ Click **Next** to continue.

Windows 95 makes it possible to enclose a document with the fax.

☞ Click the **Add File** button, if you want to do this, and select the document:

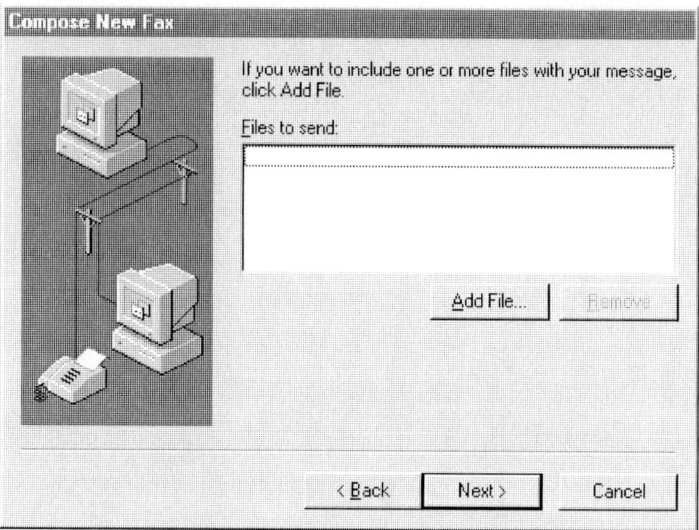

☞ Click **Next** and then **Finish** to send the fax:

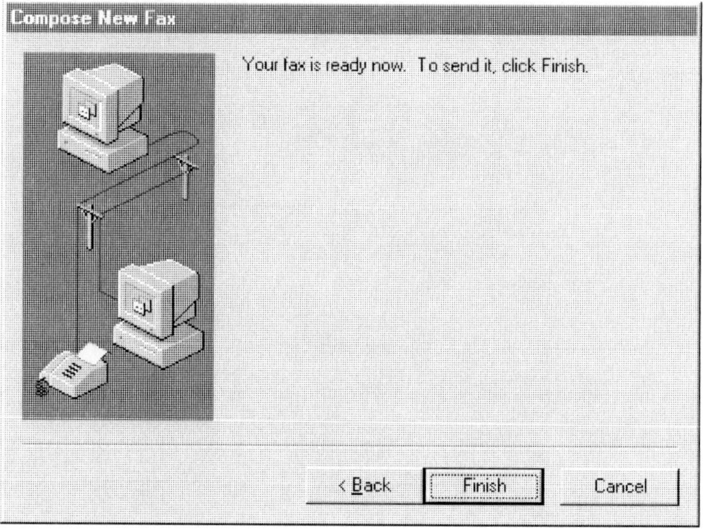

↓ personal notes ↓

5. Managing the address book

The address book contains addresses in formats which vary according to the services installed, that is to say, the different modes of transmission exploited by **Microsoft Exchange**:

- Mail postoffice addresses
- Fax addresses
- Internet addresses

In the inbox :

☞ **Tools**
Address book

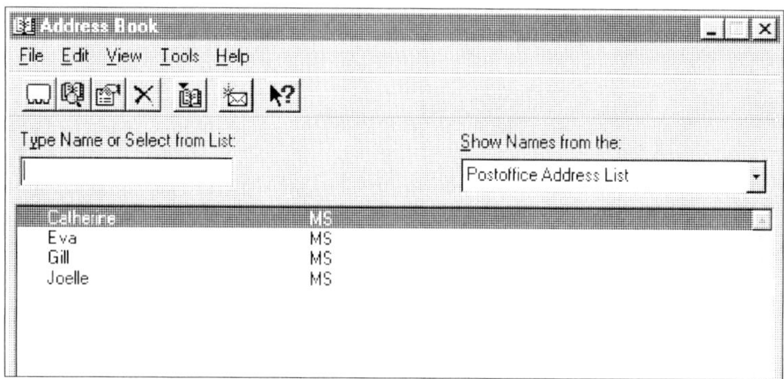

Adding a new address

To add a new address:

☞ **File**
New Entry

The **New Entry** dialog box appears. Start by choosing the type of address you want to create:

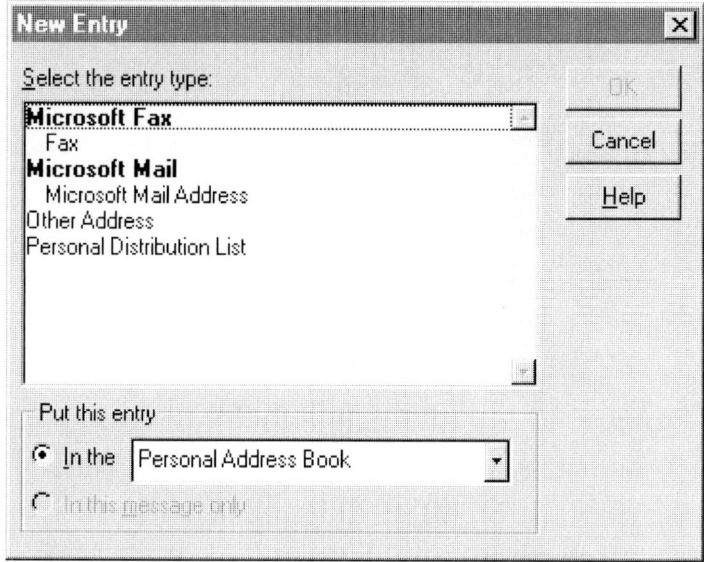

A Fax address

☞ Select **Fax** from the **New Entries** dialog box and click **OK**.

☞ In the window which appears, enter the name and fax number which make up the new address:

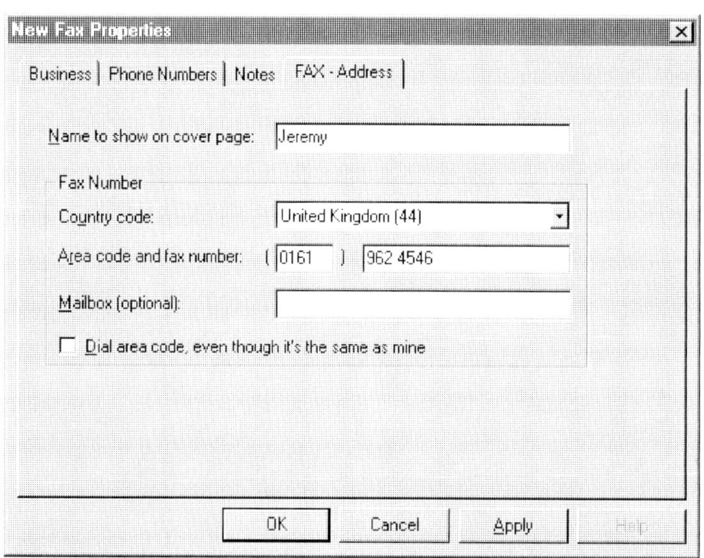

Other complementary details, such as professional co-ordinates, can be entered under the various tabs:

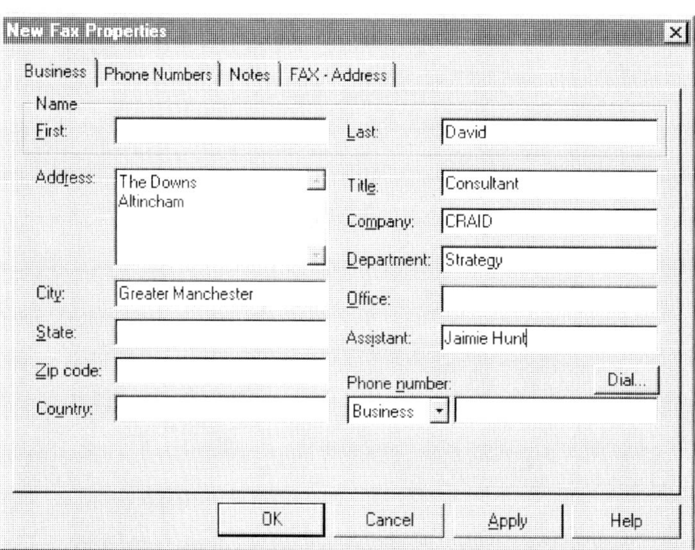

☞ Click **OK** when you have finished.

The new address is available for selection when you create a new fax.

A distribution list

This type of address is in fact a set of several recipients grouped together under a single identifier. It is used for Microsoft Exchange mail shots. If you send a message to the distribution list identifier, all the members of the list receive a copy.

To create a personal distribution list:

☞ Select the corresponding option in the **New Entry** window:

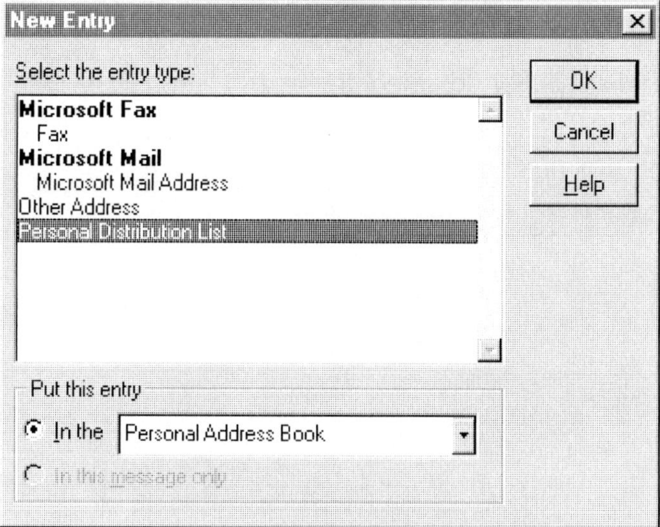

☞ Click **OK** to display the window for creating a distribution list:

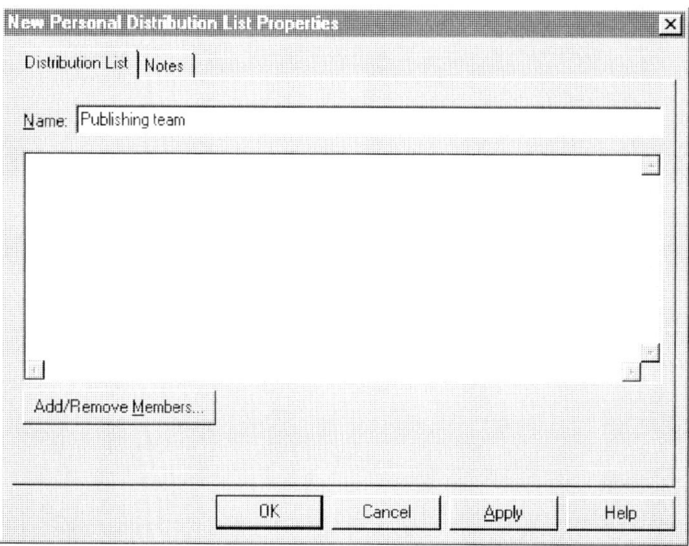

☞ Click the **Add/Remove Members** button to select the recipients to include in the list.

☞ Use the **Members** button to add names to the list.

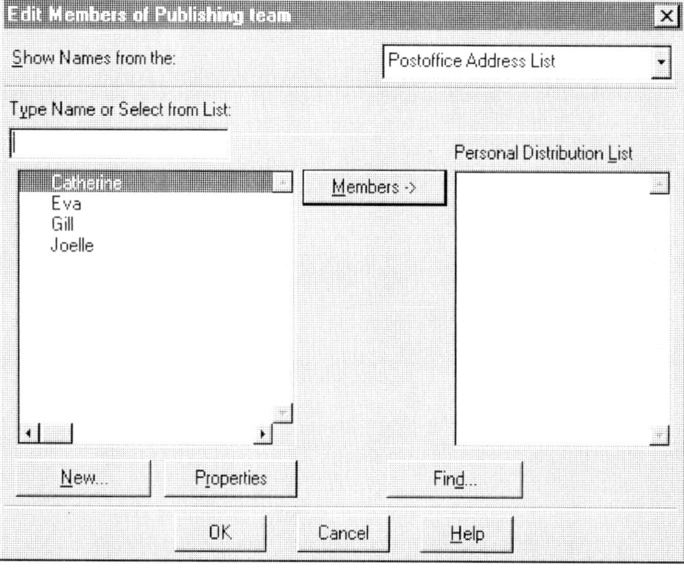

☞ When you have finished drawing up (or modifying) the distribution list, confirm by clicking **OK** twice.

A distribution list has a distinct icon in the address book and its name appears in bold characters:

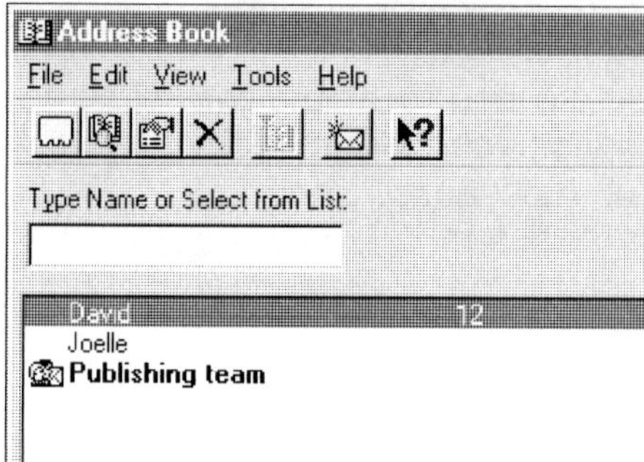

The list can include any type of address, not only fax addresses. When you are sending a message, you use the distribution list address just as if it were a normal address: Exchange simply sends the message to each of its members.

F. Configuring Microsoft Exchange

1. General options

These are accessible via the inbox's **Tools - Options** menu.

Notice the check box which can be activated to empty the **Deleted Items** folder each time you close the application. This prevents the build-up of spent messages, some of them quite large, on the disk (deleting an item in Exchange is a logical operation only: it transfers the message in question to the **Deleted Items** folder) :

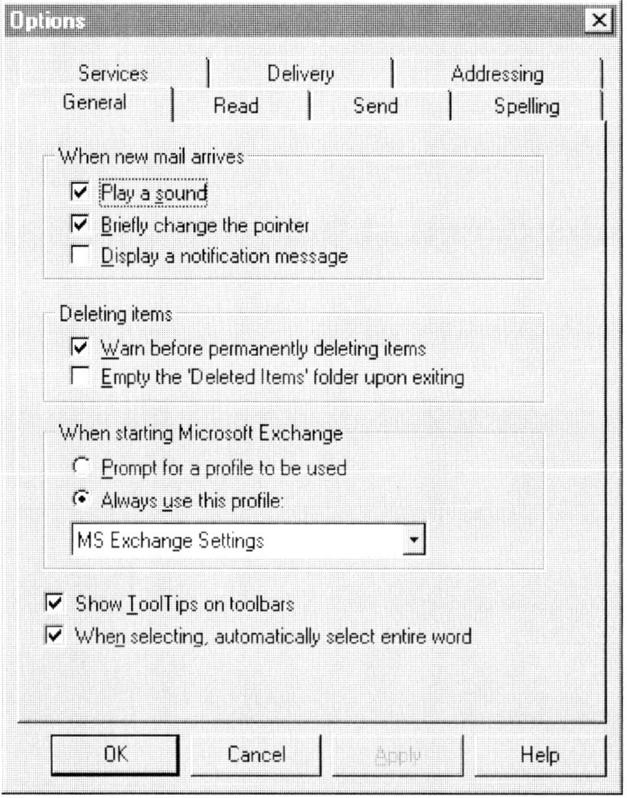

The **Services** tab of the same dialog box is also important: this is where you can add or remove transport services and configure them:

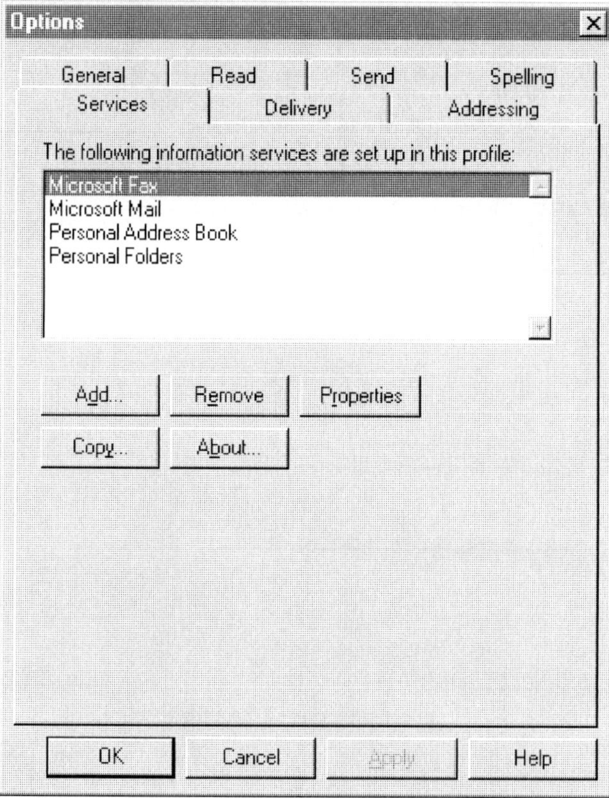

2. Configuring the Fax service

Configuring the fax service is particularly important. It defines the following settings:

– when faxes are transmitted (immediately, during off-peak hours...).

– whether or not to add a default cover page (and which one).

– the paper format and print quality to use.

– the type of dialing, the code to connect to an outside line...
– whether or not to share the fax modem with other network users.
– how the fax responds to an incoming call on the line (automatic/manual/no answer).
– the sender details (yours) which appear on the fax cover page.

Time to send and default cover page

☞ Open the inbox  .

☞ **Tools**
Services

☞ Select the **Microsoft Fax** service from the list then click the **Properties** button.

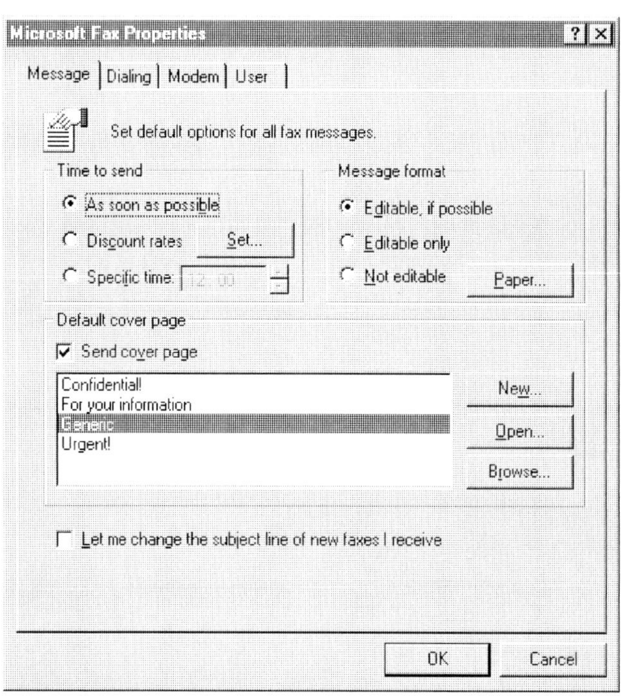

Under the **Message** tab, you can modify the settings to determine whether faxes should be sent straight away, at discount rate (click **Define** to specify the off-peak periods), or at a set time. On the same page, you can select a cover page or create a new one.

By clicking the **Paper** button, you can choose the size of the paper and the quality for printing the fax. The quality affects the *transmission speed*, that is to say the *cost* of sending the fax.

Dialing properties

☞ In the same dialog box, activate the **Dialing** tab.

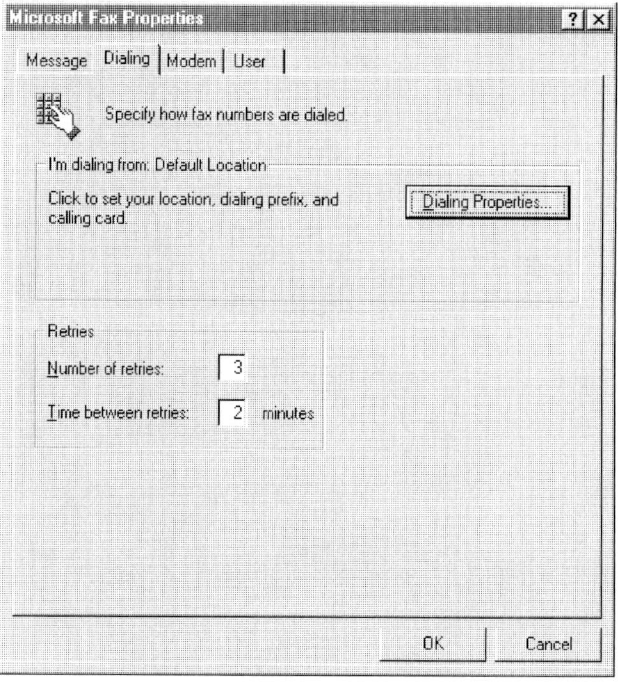

☞ Click the **Dialing Properties** button then edit the settings in the window which appears:

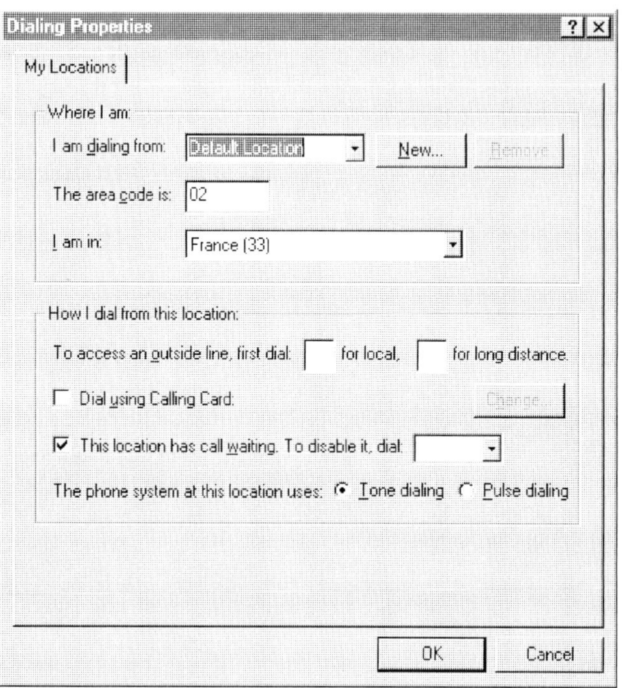

☞ Click **OK** to finish.

Sharing and answer mode

☞ Open the inbox 

.

☞ **Tools**
Services

☞ Select **Microsoft Fax** from the list of services then click the **Properties** button.

☞ Under the modem tab, activate the check box to share the fax modem and change the share name if you wish:

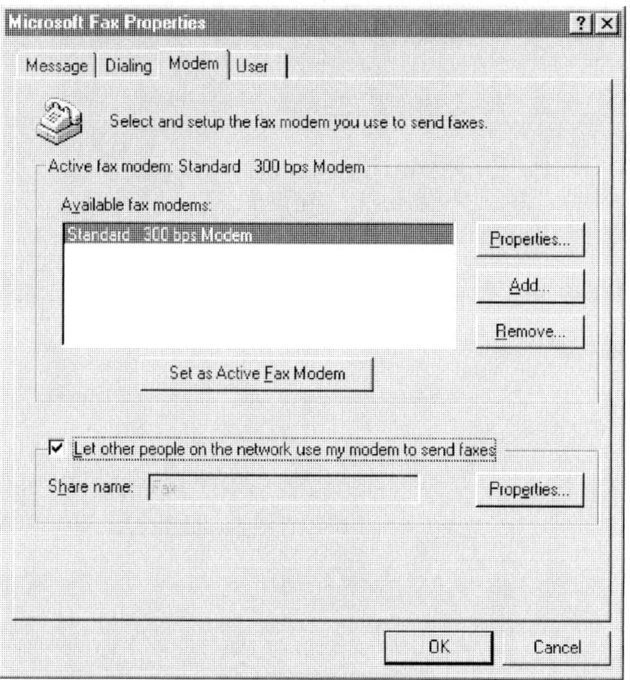

Network users can connect to a shared fax by clicking the **Add** button in the preceding dialog box and choosing **Network fax server**.

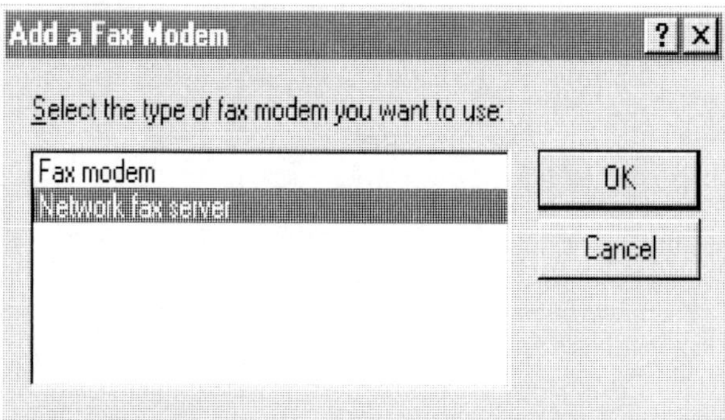

then by clicking **OK** and giving the UNC name of the shared fax directory:

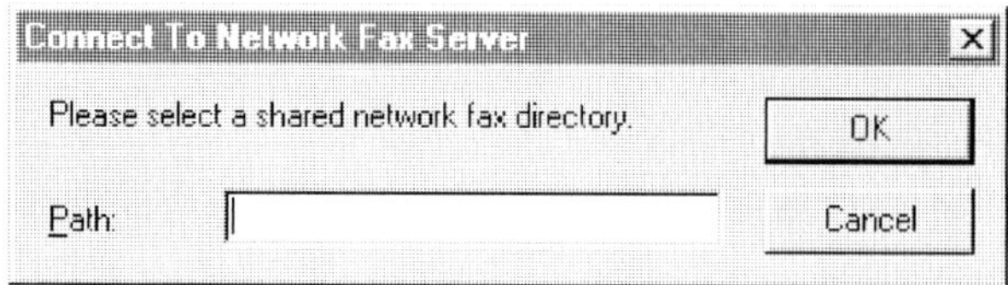

☞ You can change the answer mode for responding to an incoming fax by selecting one of the modems in the list and clicking the corresponding **Properties** button:

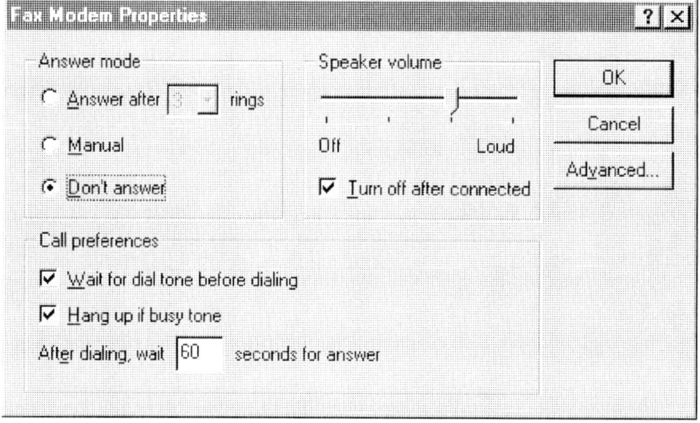

There are three possible answer modes:

- **Don't answer**,
- **Answer after x rings** answers the call automatically,
- **Manual** prompts the user to indicate whether or not to respond to the call.

This same dialog box allows you to adjust the speaker volume and to determine how the fax reacts to a busy tone.

User details on the cover page

- Open the inbox 

.
- **Tools**
  Services
- Select the Microsoft Fax service from the list and click the **Properties** button.
- Activate the **User** tab.

The dialog box which appears collects all the information which will appear on the cover page of any fax you send:

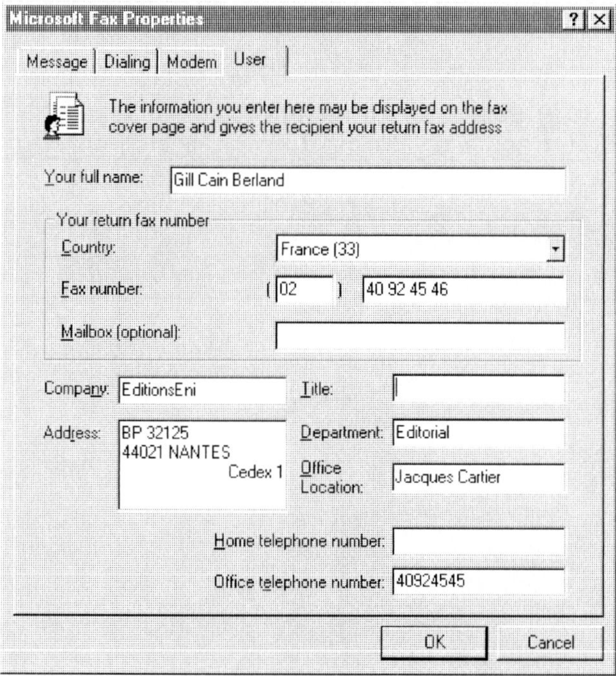

- Fill in the details and click **OK**.

3. Configuring the MSMail service

The options for configuring **MSMail** are numerous and a detailed examination of them all is beyond the scope of this book.

Among the principle settings which can be defined in the properties of the MSMail service, the *location of the postoffice* and the identity of the user are indispensable. MSMail can also be configured to run with Dial-up networking.

Postoffice location

- Open the inbox 

.
- **Tools**
  Services
- In the list of services available, select **Microsoft Mail** then click the **Properties** button and activate the **Connection** tab:

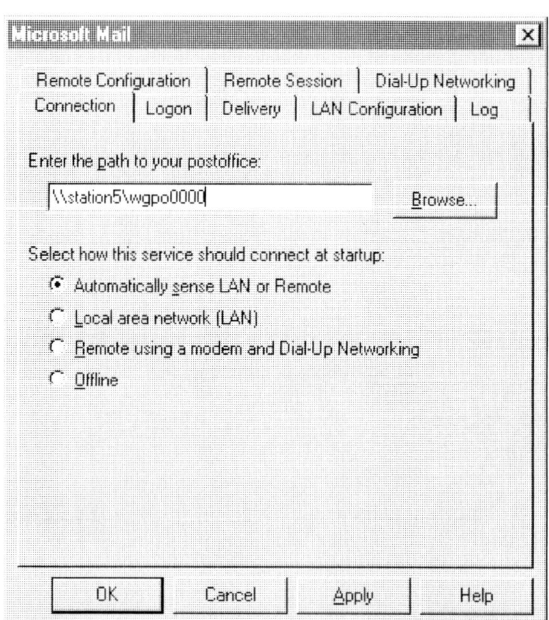

Identifying the user of MSMail

☞ In the same dialog box, activate the **Logon** tab :

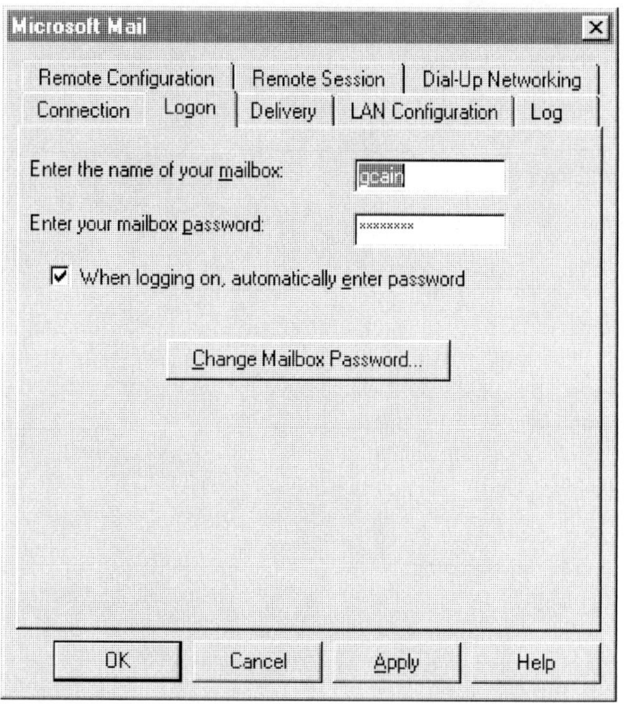

G. Structure of the postoffice hierarchy

Directory	Content
ATT	Enclosed items and encrypted files.
CAL	Calendar files from Schedule + (Office application).
FOLDERS	Public and personal folders.
GLB	SMMail's global system files, logon information.
HLP	Help files.
INF	Information files.
TPL	Template files.
KEY	Index files which contain pointers to post bag headers.
MAI	Messages stored in an encrypted form waiting to be retrieved.
MBG	Mail header pointing to the MAI files.
MEM	List of postoffice members.
MMF	Mail message files.
NME	Alias address list pointers.
P1	Temporary storage of external programs.
XTN	User for migration to Mail Server.

Mobile computing

A. The Windows 95 approach

Windows 95 is completely network orientated: it is purpose-built for both local and wide area networks. A wide range of functions facilitate the use of a portable computer which is likely to move from site to site and change its configuration. This is genuinely innovative in the current state of operating systems. Among the principle functions and tools which Windows 95 provides to simplify portable computing are:

- the *Plug and Play* configuration.
  When you are working at a portable computer which is connected on and off to a docking station, the capacity to detect new devices automatically is a great advantage (see chapter 4 *The Plug and Play standard*).
- the Dial-up networking service. This service is vital to the user on the road: it enables him or her to access the company network by means of a simple modem and exploit its disk or printer resources (see chapter 6 *The network*).
- total support for dial-up networking by *Microsoft Exchange*.
  You can run the application whether you are working with a local network or a remote one and, better still, the difference is transparent (see chapter 7 *Microsoft Exchange*).
- The remote connection by cable utility.
  This makes it possible to link two machines on a temporary basis and to transfer files or printing data (it is the successor to *Interlink*).
- My Briefcase.
  This utility provides the means of synchronising files on several disks or machines. It is discussed in detail below.
- Deferred printing.
  Print jobs can be created even if no printer is currently accessible.

B. My Briefcase

1. Description

The Briefcase deals with files that you transfer from one disk to another, or from one machine to another. It manages synchronisation between different versions of the files, proposing to reconcile the versions.

For the time being, this is just a matter of replacing an older version by a newer version, but the briefcase API leaves open the possibility of really merging two objects, if reconciliation is correctly supported by their applications.

2. How it works

Suppose a desktop computer contains a file named "Travel report" which you intend to take out on your portable computer.

The first thing to do is to drag a copy of the document from the disk of the desktop machine onto the **My Briefcase** icon. If the icon has been deleted, you can easily recreate it by means of a right-click on the desktop.

The next step is to transfer the Briefcase to the portable computer. Lastly, you need to copy the document to a location on the portable computer which is outside the Briefcase.

Now you can work on either machine and, when you have finished, copy the Briefcase onto the other.

There is no need to put the document you have modified back into the Briefcase.

To synchronise the versions of the document:

☞ Double-click the briefcase to open it.

The **Status** column indicates whether or not the document needs updating:

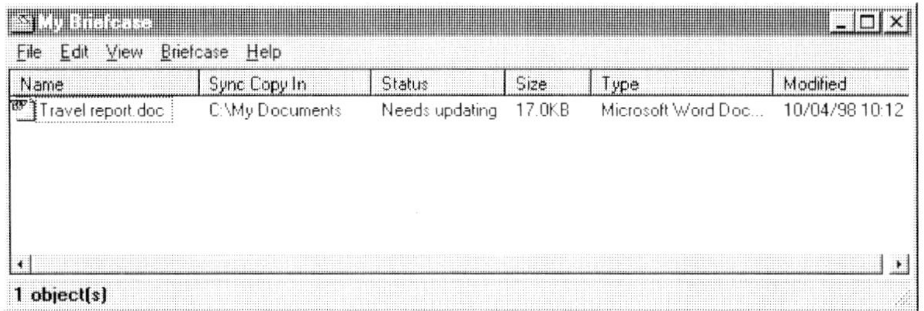

☞ **Briefcase**
Update All

The Briefcase lets you know the direction in which to copy the file:

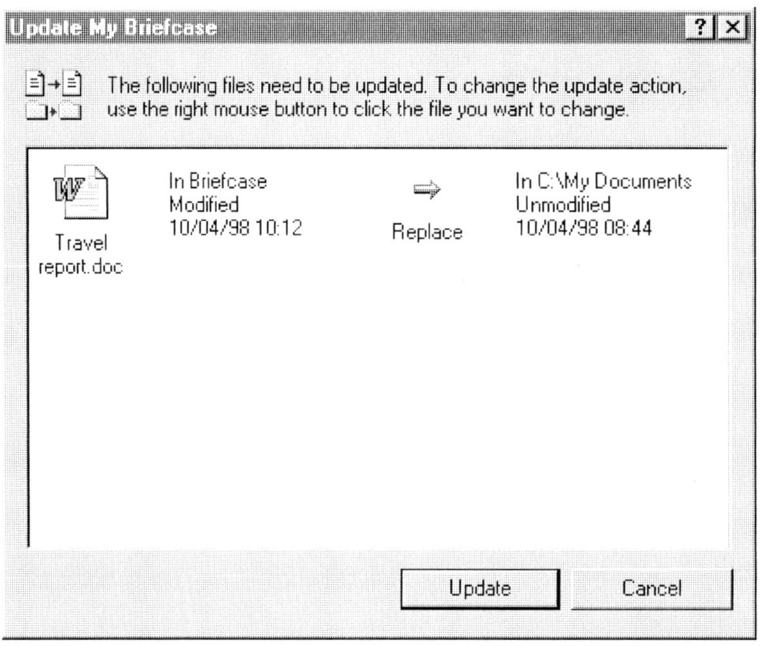

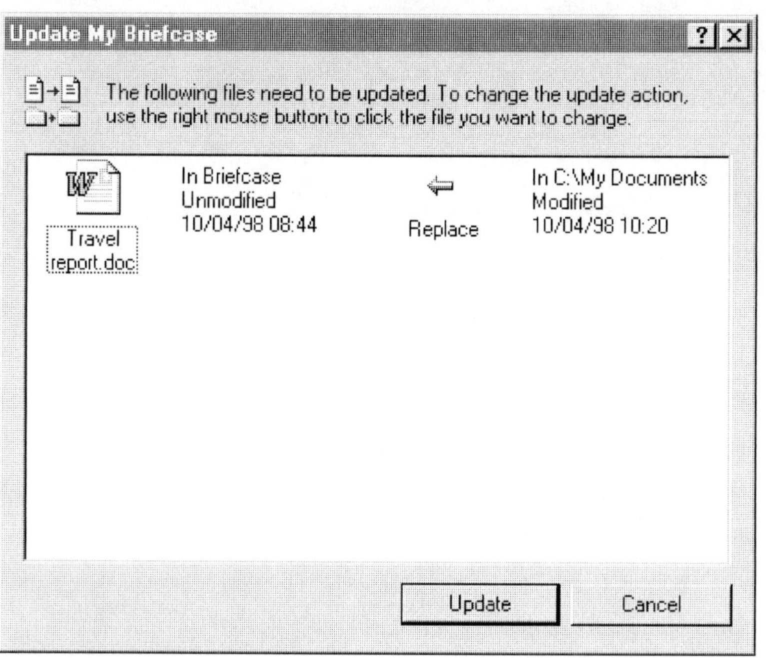

In the event that the document has been modified on both machines, the Briefcase notifies you and proposes to abandon the reconciliation:

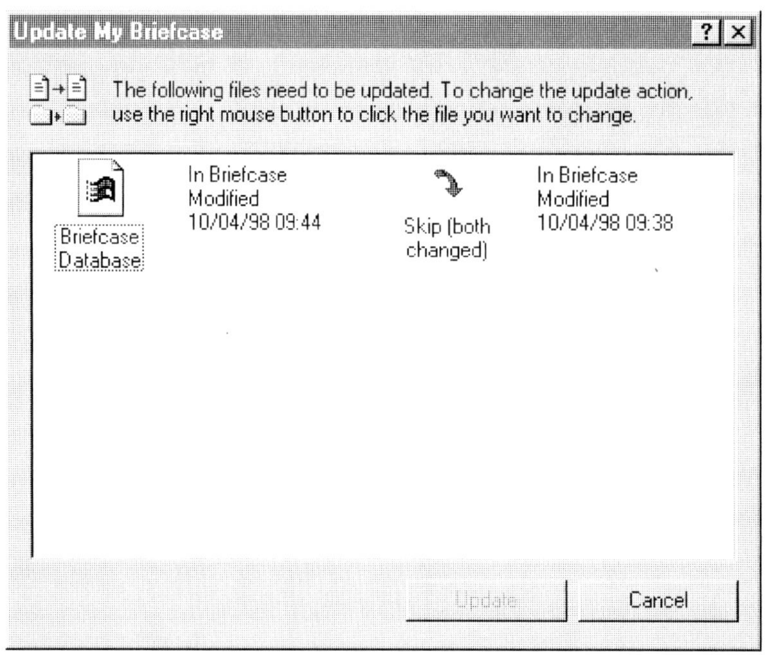

If you know which file should replace the other, right-click the icon representing the document and choose the appropriate option from the shortcut menu:

The command prompt

A. Session commands

These commands are similar to MS-DOS commands, but they take advantage of the fact that the system has been rewritten in 32 bits. Like MS-DOS commands, some of them are internal (resident in command.com) and others are external, existing as programs in the directory C:\Windows\command.

The external commands in the table below are marked with the letter (e):

attrib (e)	break	cd
chcp	chdir	chkdsk (e)
cls	command (e)	copy
ctty	date	drvspace (e)
debug (e)	defrag (e)	del
deltree (e)	dir	diskcopy (e)
doskey (e)	edit (e)	emm386 (e)
erase	exit	expand (e)
fc (e)	fdisk (e)	find (e)
for (e)	format (e)	keyb (e)
label (e)	lh	loadfix (e)
loadhigh	md	mem (e)
mkdir	mode (e)	more
move (e)	nlsfunc (e)	path
prompt	rd	ren
rename	rmdir	scandisk (e)
set	setver (e)	smartdrv (e)
sort (e)	start (e)	subst (e)
sys (e)	time	type
ver	verify	vol
xcopy (e)		

B. Commands for batch files

Used in constructing scripts, these commands constitute basic control structures which can affect the running of a program:

call	choice	echo
for	goto	if
pause	rem	shift

C. Network commands

These commands derived from commands which existed in the *LanManager* network software resemble closely the commands available in *Windows for Workgroups*. They can be used from a command-prompt session or included in a batch file, particularly a script for connecting to a server.

Net config	Net diag	Net help
Net init	Net logoff	Net logon
Net password	Net print	Net start
Net stop	Net time	Net use
Net ver	Net view	

D. Commands used in config.sys

These commands are similar to their MS-DOS counterparts. There are in addition equivalent commands which act in the upper memory area: their names end in *high*.

break	buffers	buffershigh
country	device	devicehigh
dos	drivparm	fcbs
fcbshigh	include	install
lastdrive	lastdrivehigh	menucolor
menudefault	menuitem	numlock
rem	shell	stacks
stackshigh	submenu	switches

E. Drivers for installing in config.sys

Their role has not changed since MS-DOS and they are still installed by the command **DEVICE=** or **DEVICEHIGH=**. They are located either in the WINDOWS directory or in the WINDOWS\COMMAND subdirectory.

display.sys	driver.sys	emm386.exe
himem.sys	keyboard.sys	mscdex.exe
ansi.sys		

F. TCP/IP commands and utilities

Available after the installation of TCP/IP, these commands enable the provision of connectivity services, print services... for UNIX machines.

ARP	Protocol managing IP-ETHERNET address resolution tables.
Ftp	Protocol and command for transferring binary or ASCII files.
Nbtstat	Diagnostics and statistics on connections which useNetBIOS over TCP/IP.
Netstat	Diagnostic and statistics on connections which use TCP/IP.
Ping	Diagnostic command for connection to a remote machine (time there and back for an ICMP packet).
Route	Command for managing routing tables.
Telnet	Protocole and command for terminal emulation via TCP/IP.
Tracert	Diagnostic command which tests routing by sending an ICMP packet.

↓ personal notes ↓

The registry editor

A. Definition of the registry

The Windows 95 registry is a hierarchical database which stores all the data relating to hardware and software configurations in Windows.

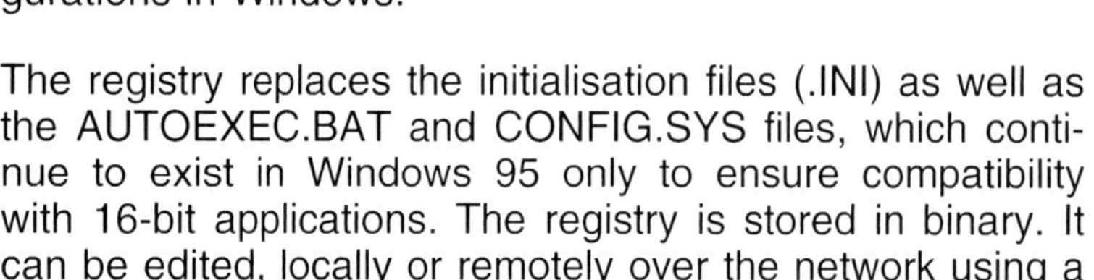

The registry replaces the initialisation files (.INI) as well as the AUTOEXEC.BAT and CONFIG.SYS files, which continue to exist in Windows 95 only to ensure compatibility with 16-bit applications. The registry is stored in binary. It can be edited, locally or remotely over the network using a purpose-built utility: the registry editor. This utility's path is \WINDOWS\REGEDIT.EXE.

B. Sources of registry data

The Windows 95 registry is *dynamic*. This is fundamental to understanding how it works. It also explains why it is impossible to give a full description of its contents, which vary from one machine to another, or from one moment to the next.

There are several sources which supply data to the registry:

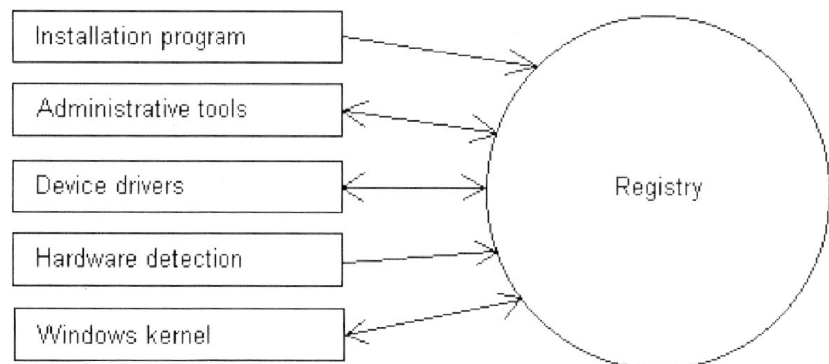

The installation program

The first time you install Windows 95 and again each time you add or remove components, the configuration manager edits the registry to update the configuration data there.

Administrative tools

System policies or the profiles editor can write in the registry to store information about user's permissions, or conversely, they can obtain this type of information from the registry.

Device drivers

Device drivers can obtain settings from the registry or write configuration data there. In this respect, the registry plays the same role as the CONFIG.SYS file in MS-Dos.

The Windows kernel

This stores in the registry information about the version of Windows. It also uses the registry to store a series of dynamic items of data as it is loading.

Hardware detection

Each time a new piece of hardware is detected, configuration information is added to the registry. The Plug and Play system adds a lot of data to the registry.

C. Structure of the Windows 95 registry

The registry is divided into keys, these are organised into a hierarchy along the following lines:

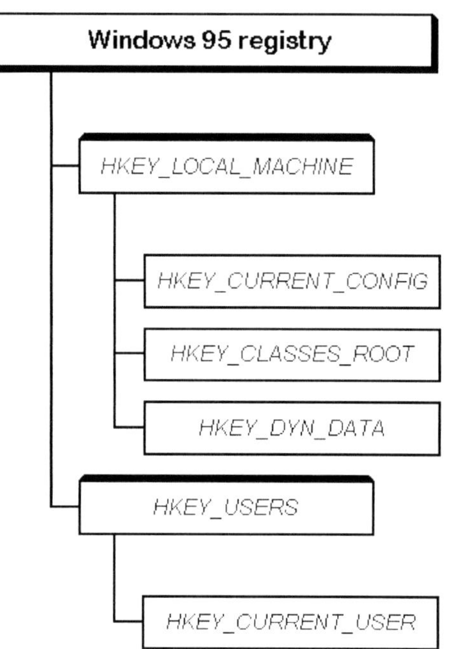

- HKEY_LOCAL_MACHINE
  This key contains all the settings concerning the hardware and software configuration of the computer where Windows 95 is installed.
- HKEY_CURRENT_CONFIG
  Since Windows 95 can save and use different hardware configurations, this key contains the configuration currently in use. It is a subkey of HKEY_LOCAL_MACHINE.

- HKEY_CLASSES_ROOT
  This key contains all the file extensions and their associations with applications. It is exploited in the implementation of OLE functions. For example, when you drag a document to a printer shortcut the document's source application starts automatically because the application is associated with the extension of the document.
- HKEY_DYN_DATA
  This key contains dynamic configuration data, indicating the status of certain Plug and Play devices which are added and removed dynamically.
- HKEY_USERS
  This key contains all the information concerning the various users who exist in the system (profiles). It supplies standard parameters for new users as well as settings for all those already created: appearance of the desktop, default application parameters...
- HKEY_CURRENT_USER
  This subkey of HKEY_USERS contains data specific to the user who is currently logged on.

D. Files which constitute the registry

The registry is essentially composed of two files:

SYSTEM.DAT is located in the Windows directory. It contains data relating to the hardware and software configuration of the machine.

USER.DAT contains user information. Depending on the configuration selected, this file is located in the WINDOWS directory or, if local profiles are active, in the \Windows\profiles\user directory. If profiles on the server are in use, it can also be situated on another computer on the network.

Each time Windows 95 starts correctly, the system makes copies of USER.DAT and SYSTEM.DAT named USER.DA0 and SYSTEM.DA0. If a problem occurs at startup, the system can copy these two files onto the current registry so that it can start without difficulty.

E. The registry editor

This program, named **REGEDIT.EXE**, does not appear in any of the Windows 95 menus. To start it:

☞ **Start**
Run

☞ Type in REGEDIT then enter.

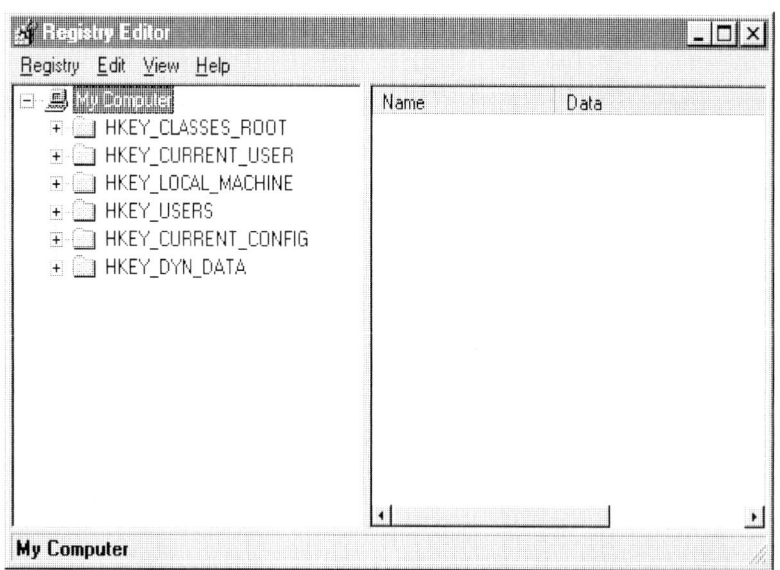

Editing a registry key is an exceptional operation which should only be undertaken with the greatest possible caution. An error in the registry can seriously impair the running of Windows.

For each registry key, there is a corresponding set of values which may be binary (symbolised by the icon) or alphanumerical (symbolised by the icon):

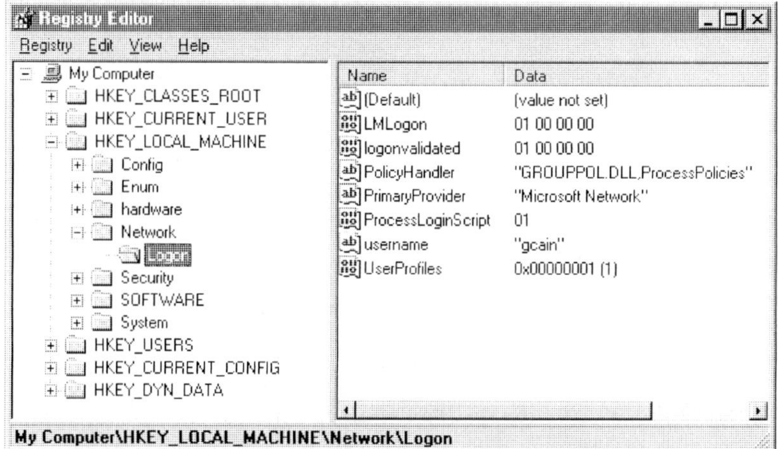

To edit a value:

☞ Double-click the value. In this example, the value *User-Name* is being edited:

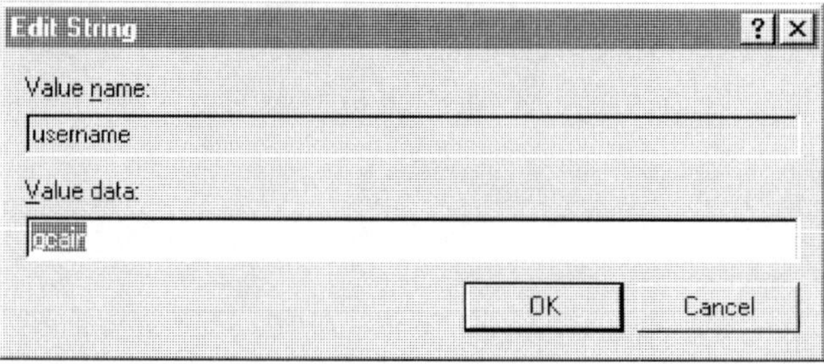

↓ personal notes ↓

F. Opening the registry from a remote machine

It is possible to open and consult the registry of another machine on the network. For this, the two machines must be configured to:

- apply *user level security*: this implies that they must be members of an NT Server *domain* (Control Panel - Network),
- authorise remote administration (Control Panel - Password),
- run the remote registry service.

The service is not installed by default in Windows 95. Moreover, *it is only supplied in the CD ROM version.*

The first stage in opening a remote registry, then, is to install the service:

☞ Right-click the 

and display its **Properties**.

☞ Click the **Add** button and select **Service** from the list:

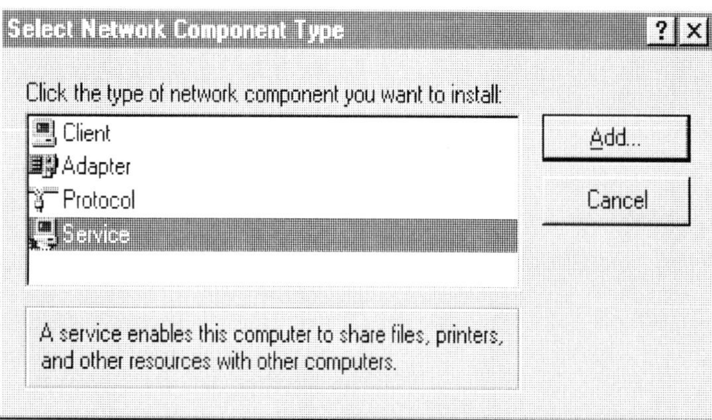

☞ Click **Add** again and then the **Have Disk** button.

- Give the path to the \ADMIN\NETTOOLS\REMOTE-REG directory on the Windows 95 CD-ROM then click **OK**.

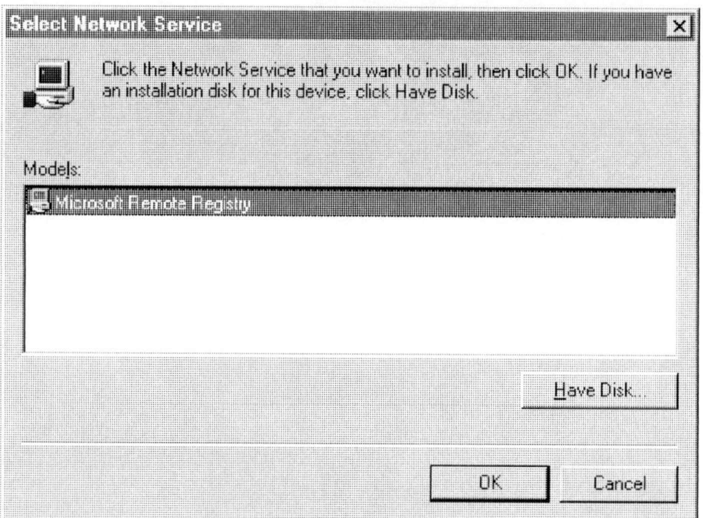

Windows proposes to install the remote registry service: click **OK** to accept.

- When the installation is complete, restart the computer.
- Go through the same procedure on the second machine.

You can now open and edit the remote registry by the menu command:

Registry
Connect Network Registry

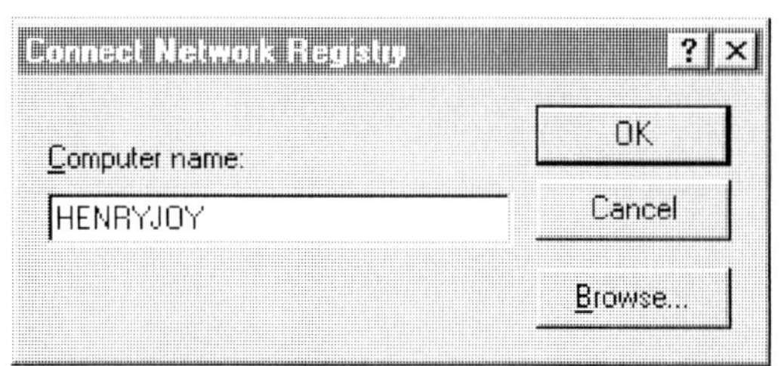

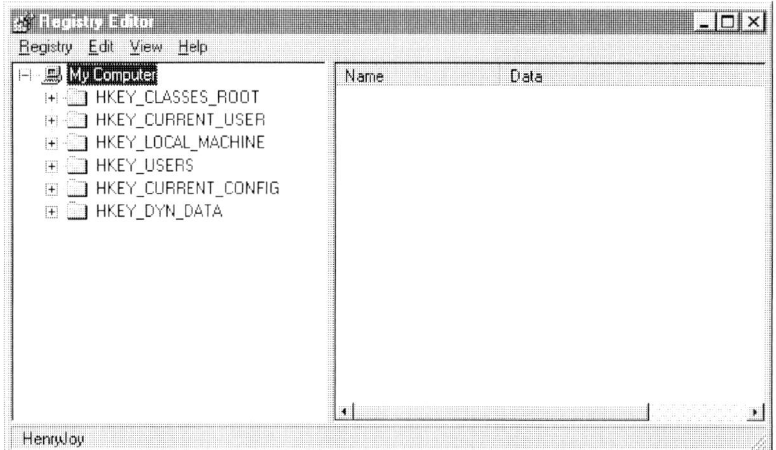

Troubleshooting

The first step in ensuring that your computer can be repaired easily is to back up the registry, which is stored in the files SYSTEM.DAT and USER.DAT.

Apart from that, you should keep a system startup disk so that the essential files of Windows can be reinstalled if there is a major crash.

A. Creating a startup disk

You must have a system disk to restart the computer if there has been a serious problem, for instance, the destruction of a vital system file or a viral attack.

In no circumstances can you use an MS-DOS disk instead, because the two sets of system files are fundamentally *different*.

You can create the disk by means of a series of SYS A:, commands followed by a copy of the appropriate files, or by an easy, interactive method.

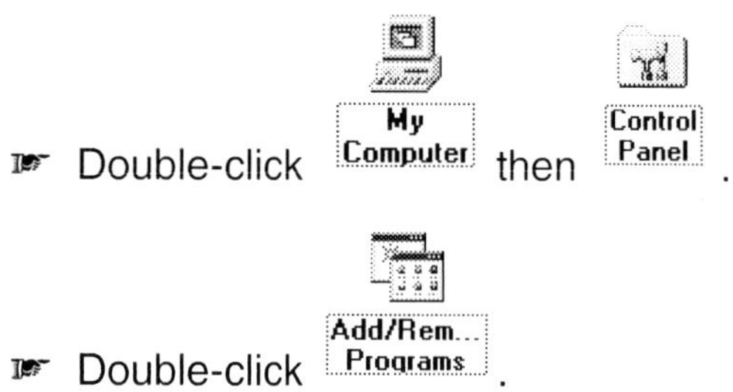

☞ Double-click My Computer then Control Panel.

☞ Double-click Add/Rem... Programs.

☞ Choose the **Startup disk** tab.

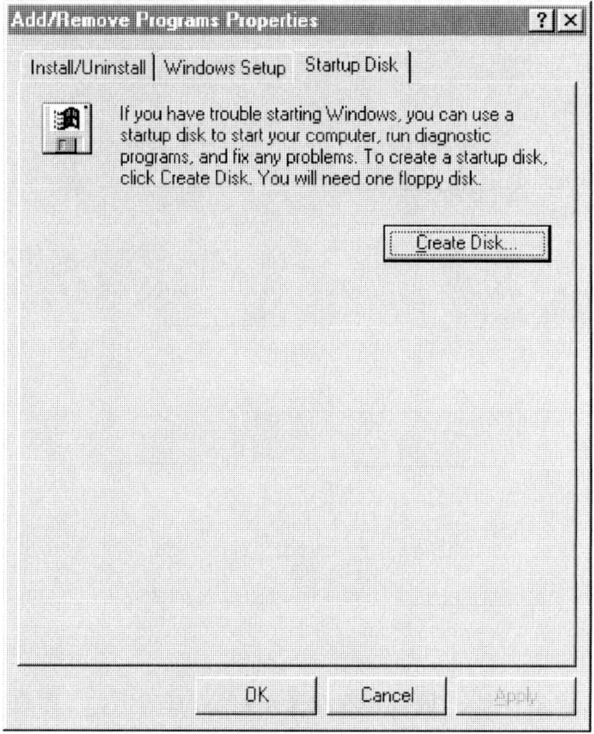

☞ Click the **Create Disk** button.

The system starts to create the disk.

B. Logs

1. Automatic logs

Windows 95 automatically keeps a number of logs in the form of ASCII files. These make it possible to monitor the running of the system and to detect a certain number of faults:

Log	Contents
C:\BOOTLOG.TXT	records concerning boot operations (similar to the log file in versions 3.x of Windows).
C:\DETLOG.TXT	records concerning the devices detected at installation.
C:\SETUPLOG.TXT	installation messages.
C:\WINDOWS\IOS.LOG	error messages from SCSI drivers.

2. The modem log

The activity of the modem can also be logged. Unlike the logs listed above, this one is not kept automatically: it needs to be activated by the user:

☞ Double-click My Computer then Control Panel.

☞ Choose 
Modems
.

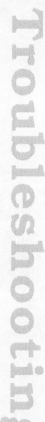

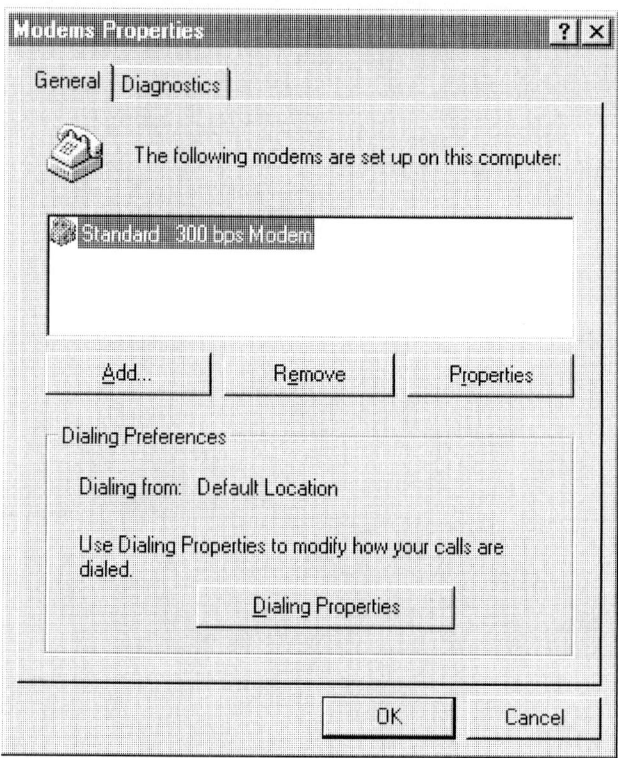
Modems Properties
General
Diagnostics
The following modems are set up on this computer:
Standard 300 bps Modem
Add...
Remove
Properties
Dialing Preferences
Dialing from: Default Location
Use Dialing Properties to modify how your calls are dialed.
Dialing Properties
OK
Cancel

☞ Click the **Properties** button.

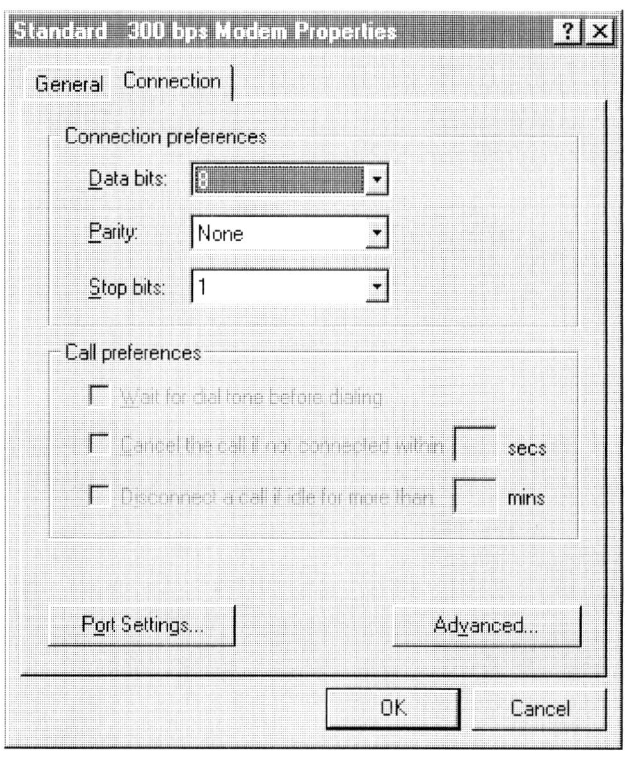

☞ Click the **Advanced** button and on the screen which appears activate the check box which initialises the log **MODEMLOG.TXT**:

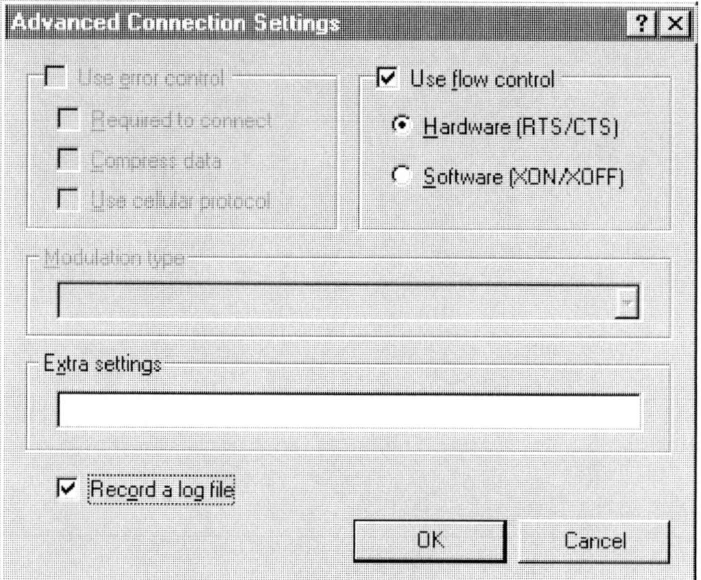

☞ Click **OK** to enter.

The next time the modem is used, the MODEMLOG.TXT file will be created in the Windows directory, listing any problems encountered.

Extract from a MODEMLOG.TXT file:

```
12-13-1995 15:22:32.37 - Standard 300 bps Modem
in use.
12-13-1995 15:22:32.49 - Modem type: Standard
300 bps Modem FAX extern
12-13-1995 15:22:32.49 - Modem inf path:
MDMUSRG.INF
12-13-1995 15:22:32.49 - Modem inf section: Modem19
12-13-1995 15:22:32.75 - 19200,N,8,1
12-13-1995 15:22:32.81 - 19200,N,8,1
12-13-1995 15:22:32.81 - 19200,N,8,1
12-13-1995 15:22:32.81 - Initializing modem.
12-13-1995 15:22:32.81 - Send: AT
12-13-1995 15:22:34.83 - ERROR: Unable to send
command to the device.
12-13-1995 15:22:35.84 - Session Statistics:
12-13-1995 15:22:35.84 - Reads: 0 bytes
12-13-1995 15:22:35.84 - Writes: 3 bytes
12-13-1995 15:22:35.84 - Standard 300 bps Modem
closed.
```

A log is also kept of remote Mail accesses.

C. Starting in safe mode

If you meet a problem to do with the installation of a device driver, in particular the driver of a video device, you can start Windows in safe mode. In this mode, only the basic system drivers are loaded. If you wish, safe mode can implement network settings.

To go into safe mode, start the computer and when the system displays the message *Starting Windows 95*, press the F8 key. A menu is produced for you to choose the type of startup you require. The F5 and F6 keys respectively start Windows in safe mode and in safe mode with network support.

Once your system is running, you can deactivate or remove the driver which is causing the problem. An indicator in each corner of the screen reminds you that the system is in safe mode.

It is also possible to load drivers in Step-by-Step mode, so that errant drivers can be neutralised.

D. Problems linked to the hard disk

You should bear in mind that most Windows applications and all printing processes create temporary files on the hard disk. These can take up a lot of space.

A lack of space on the disk can cause problems.

If the running of an application is abruptly interrupted, it can leave temporary files on the disk, in the directory C:\TEMP or C:\WINDOWS\TEMP. You should remove any remaining temporary files regularly, as they can interfere with the optimal running of the computer.

The SCANDISK utility checks the coherence of the file system. You should use it as often as possible. Another thing you should do as often as possible is to run a defragmentation of the disk: the system informs you of any problems it meets during the process.

You should never run defragmenters or repair tools other than those supplied with Windows 95 or custom-built for it: you should certainly never use DOS tools !

↓ personal notes ↓

Appendices

A. Parameters of the file MSDOS.SYS

The file MSDos.sys, which is a text file, must have a length greater than 1024 bytes. This is why some of its lines contain x characters.

1. The (Paths) section

There are three entries:

Entry	Possibles values	Description	Default value
HostWinBootDrv		the startup disk drive	C
WinBootDir		the location of the files necessary for starting Windows	C:\Windows
WinDir		the directory where Windows 95 is installed	C:\Windows

2. The (Options) section

This section can contain the following entries:

Entry	Possible values	Entry	Default value
BootDelay	number of seconds	sets the length of the pause before startup which allows you to press F8 to obtain the menu	2
BootFailSafe	0 1	starts the system in safe mode or not	0
BootGuy	0 1	activates automatic graphic startup	1
BootKeys	0 1	activates startup keys or not (F5,F6,F8)	1
BootMenu	0 1	automatically displays the boot menu: value 1 is equivalent to pressing F8 at startup	0
BootMenuDefault	1 to chosen number in the menu	sets the default choice form the menu	3 for a machine which is not in a network otherwise 4

Appendices

↓ personal notes ↓

Entry	Possible values	Entry	Default value
BootMenuDelay	number of seconds	defines the length of the pause before the default choice in the menu is taken	30
BootMulti	0 1	activates a dual MS-DOS/ Windows 95 boot	0
BootWarn	0 1	activates warning and start menu in safe mode	1
BootWin	0 1	selects Windows 95 as the default system on a machine which can start in dual boot mode (MS-DOS installed)	1
DblSpace	0 1	automatically loads dblspace.bin	1
DoubleBuffer	0 1	uses a double buffer for SCSI controllers or not	1
DrvSpace	0 1	automatically loads DrvSpace.bin	1
LoadTop	0 1	loads command.com and DrvSpace.bin at the top of the 640 Kb	1

Entry	Possible values	Entry	Default value
Logo	0 1	displays the logo	1
NetWork	0 1	includes in the start menu an option "safe mode with network support"	1 if network installed otherwise 0

B. Startup function keys

Key	Description
F4	runs the previously installed version of MS-Dos
F5	starts the system in safe mode
⇧ Shift F5	starts the system in safe mode command prompt only
F6	starts the system in safe mode with network support
F8	displays the Windows 95 startup menu

C. Parameters of the Extract program

Extract is a program for extracting individual Windows 95 files for their cabinets (.CAB files):

– extract /Y *compressed_file destination_file*

– extract [/Y] [/A] [/D /E] [/L *location*] *cabinet_file* [*file specification*]

Option	Description
/A	processes all the cabinet files from *cabinet_file* onwards
/D	supplies a list of directories: does not extract
/E	enforced extraction
/L	extracts in the specified location instead of in the current directory
/y	overwrites the files in the destination directory without asking for confirmation
compressed_file	cabinet file containing just one compressed file
destination_file	location and name of the destination file
cabinet_file	cabinet fiel containing several compressed files
file_specification	indication including wildcard characters specifying the files to extract, *.* for example

Index

A